Reclaiming the Lutheran Liturgical Heritage

BLUE PAPERS • VOLUME 1
MARK LUTHER JOHNSON • SERIES EDITOR

Reclaiming the Lutheran Liturgical Heritage

by

Oliver K. Olson

Introduction by Gracia Grindal

Reclaiming the Lutheran Liturgical Heritage
Oliver K. Olson

Introduction by Gracia Grindal

First printing April 2007

Copyright © 2007 ReClaim Resources

Except for brief quotations in critical articles or reviews, no part of this book may be reproduced in any manner, printed, electronic, or otherwise, without prior written permission from the publishers or copyright holders. Write to: Permissions, Reclaim Resources, PO Box 8202, Saint Paul, Minn. 55108

ISBN 1-932458-55-7

For more information on ReClaim Resources, visit **www.ReClaimLutheranWorship.org**

Published by Bronze Bow Publishing LLC, 2600 E. 26th Street, Minneapolis, Minn. 55406

www.bronzebowpublishing.com

This book was designed and set in type by Koechel Peterson and Associates, Inc., Minneapolis, Minn. Publication of this book made possible by contributions from many individuals, households, and groups.

Manufactured in the U.S.A.

10 9 8 7 6 5 4 3 2

Contents

Preface 1

Introduction 3

1   Christ's Command, "Do This" 13

2   Liturgical Novelties 23

3   The Lord's Supper 29

4   The Church's Supper 43

5   Ecumenical Authority? 53

6   The Eucharistic Prayer 65

7   Reclaiming Christ's Testament 79

Abbreviations 87

Glossary 88

Acknowledgments: Mark Luther Johnson, Blue Papers Editor; Gracia Grindal, Editor-in-Chief, ReClaim Resources; Carolyn Lystig, Managing Editor. Editorial Assistants: Daniel D. Baker, Sarah S. Johnson, Norman P. Olsen, Rosalie Rosholt, Pamela Schwandt. Photographs courtesy of O. K. Olson, 16; S. S. Johnson, 39; Hilary N. Bullock, back cover.

Preface

More than thirty-five years ago, Oliver Olson defended an interpretation of liturgy that grounded itself in the principles of the Reformation.[1] Olson called into question the then dominant trend to privilege liturgical practices of the fifth and sixth centuries as filtered through specious historical and theological arguments of scholars motivated by an anti-Protestant ideology.

A few years later, his arguments were recognized as valid by a preeminent Anglican liturgical scholar, Bryan Spinks of Cambridge University[2]; not that it made any difference to those Lutherans who have controlled the preparation of worship materials for the ELCA and its predecessor bodies.

For students who care about Lutheran identity and worship practice, however, Oliver Olson is a gift to the church and an inexhaustible resource. The modest book that you hold in your hand is the fruit of a half century of scholarly study distilled into a relatively few pages of historical observations, suggestions, and principles. It is written in a way that is comprehensible to the beginning student in the field.

Walter Sundberg

[1] Oliver K. Olson, "Contemporary Trends in Liturgy Viewed from the Perspective of Classical Lutheran Theology," *Lutheran Quarterly* (Old Series) 26 (1974): 110-157.

[2] Bryan Spinks, *Luther's Liturgical Criteria and His Reform of the Canon of the Mass* (Bramcote Notte: Grove Books, 1982), 40.

Introduction by Gracia Grindal

The book you have in your hand is a miracle, one that has been aborning for more than fifty years, if not since the Reformation. The writer, Dr. Oliver K. Olson, has been a lone voice in the liturgical life of the Lutheran church for years. Ever since the modern liturgical revival swept the Western church during the middle of the last century, Olson has watched closely as Lutherans of all stripes have been carried along by the revival and the ecumenical strategy it contained: that the way to achieve unity among Christians was to construct a common liturgy that all mainline Protestants and Roman Catholics could share, and thus draw closer as Christendom faded.

> [Some thought] ... the way to achieve unity among Christians was to construct a common liturgy that all mainline Protestants and Roman Catholics could share ...

End Run Around the Reformation

This common liturgy, based on liturgies from the fourth century, would be able to make an end run around the Reformation and Luther's difficulties with the mass as a sacrifice. It could return us to a time when theological and liturgical differences among Christians supposedly did not exist. It would dispel the need for opposing liturgical traditions and mean for Lutherans that the insights of Luther could be disregarded as a historical oddity, the eucharistic prayer that Luther had removed could be restored, and Lutheran worship could be brought into line with the ecumenical liturgy of the western church.

Restoration of Eucharistic Prayer in *SBH*

The move to restore the eucharistic prayer in our day had already begun in the *Service Book and Hymnal* (*SBH*) when a Lutheran hymnal committee had returned the eucharistic prayer to the service on the dubious notion that they could see the liturgical issues at hand more clearly than Luther had in his own conflicted time.

This is apparent in the work of Luther Dotterer Reed (1873–1972) of Philadelphia's Mount Airy Seminary, a learned pastor, who as chair of the *SBH* committee, restored the eucharistic prayer, or "The Prayer of Thanksgiving," to the service (*SBH*, 34, 62).

From their vantage point, Reed and his followers thought that it was possible to see more clearly than Luther had what was at stake in his reform of the mass.

> A vision clearer than was sometimes possible in the turmoil of the Reformation controversy has revealed the enduring value of some elements which were lost temporarily in the sixteenth century reconstruction of the liturgy, as, for instance, the proper use of the prayer of thanksgiving and the essential meaning of the term 'catholic' in the creeds. (*SBH*, vii)

Clearly, Martin Luther had come to be thought of as a liturgical hack who did not know what he was doing in his excising of the canon of the mass from his revision of the mass, one way of dismissing his work. Oliver in his studies came to believe that Luther knew exactly what he was doing. For Olson it was a simple matter of the direction of the service—up or down. God was the actor, coming down to us in word and sacrament.

The eucharistic prayer and other restorations Lutheran liturgists in this country began hankering after were from us to God—the focus was on our work, or sacrifice.

Vatican II and the Beginning of *LBW*

In the 1960s when the liturgical revival of Vatican II began influencing Lutherans, Lutherans embarked on a revision of their liturgy, ostensibly updating the language, but really creating a new order of worship that they claimed would "restore" the Lutheran liturgy to the glory it had lost with Martin Luther's reform in the sixteenthth century.

Lutherans have traditionally never devoted much systematic study to issues surrounding worship, handing off the teaching of worship and the making of liturgies to the practical theologians who had been effective liturgical leaders in their own congregations. These pastors found it difficult to resist the call of both the ecumenical and liturgical movements exploding around them. They were defenseless against Vatican II because there had not really been a systematic study of liturgy grounded in Lutheran theology and practice they could access. They had to go elsewhere for their studies. This has had continuing consequences in Lutheran liturgical life.

> **Lutherans have traditionally never devoted much systematic study to issues surrounding worship, handing off the teaching of worship and the making of liturgies to the practical theologians …**

Flacius Saved the Lutheran Movement

Olson's doctoral work on the great, but lesser known Reformer, Matthias Flacius (1520–1575) and his later biography had led him to understand how significant Luther's reform of the mass was to the preservation of Lutheran theology and practice. Not many others could access this material because it was not well-known to contemporary Americans until Oliver's work. Not even *The Encyclopedia of the Lutheran Church* (Augsburg, 1965), in its entry on Flacius, explains fully the nature of the Adiaphorist Controversy in 1548, a dispute that nearly lost the Reformation for the Lutherans.

Those wanting to make peace between the warring parties (disputes between Catholics and Lutherans, and disputes among Lutherans) supported the Imperial Interim Law of 1548 (also known as the Augsburg Interim). Supporters of the law were convinced and argued that practices like the inclusion of the eucharistic prayer and other fundamental doctrines such as justification "by faith alone" could be considered *adiaphora*. They insisted that we are saved by faith *primarily* and not by faith alone.

Flacius, who came to be known as the first Gnesio-Lutheran (i.e., true or genuine Lutheran), fought this battle fiercely and, among other things, retained the theology that we are saved by faith alone. He also kept Luther's revision of the mass.

If Flacius had not advocated for retaining Luther's revision of the mass, the difference between Catholics and Lutherans liturgically would have been unnoticeable to the average lay person, who would have soon thought there was no difference between the two confessions. Flacius saw that it was through such a compromise on liturgical practices, for example, that the wolf of heresy would come through the back door. Not knowing this history or valuing it made it possible for so-called Lutheran liturgical experts to adopt practices that Lutherans had traditionally opposed.

The Way We Pray Becomes the Way We Believe

One of the fundamental texts of the new liturgical revival sweeping the churches was Dom Gregory Dix's *The Shape of the Liturgy* (Westminster, England: Dacre Press, 1945) with its romantic depiction of the services of the early church, the baptismal mysteries readying the catechumens for induction into the mysteries of the table on Easter eve, which ravished many a young mind in the 1960s.

When Vatican II had concluded in 1965, Lutherans who had wearied of the deep divisions of Christians over the five centuries since the Reformation conceived an almost physical longing for reunion with Rome.

For them, the ecumenical and liturgical movements were one and the same. If they could produce a liturgy that was pre-Constantinian, with the four-action shape suggested by Dix, they could return to a time when the church was one.

> **Flacius saw that it was through such a compromise on liturgical practices, for example, that the wolf of heresy would come through the back door.**

A liturgy could accomplish what no amount of theological or ecumenical discussion could. *Lex orandi, lex credendi*—as the people pray so they believe.

Changing the Direction

As the Inter-Lutheran Commission on Worship (ILCW) began its work in the mid-sixties, it included all three major Lutheran bodies in America—the American Lutheran Church (ALC), the Lutheran Church in America (LCA), and the Lutheran Church–Missouri Synod (LC–MS). The ecumenical excitement was almost palpable. Finally, Lutherans of their generation, who had wearied of their ethnic and theological divisions, could say they had forged a new church for all Lutherans in America and had produced a liturgy that was ecumenical.

This meant they could restore the eucharistic prayer (or at least a variation of it), move toward including the *epiclesis* (the prayer to the Holy Spirit over the elements and baptismal water), and make the offertory procession with the bringing of the gifts an ideal that they hoped some day would be universal in Lutheran worship. In other words, change the direction from God's work to ours.

Churches Consider Olson's Critique

Traditional Lutherans could not make an argument against these practices, given the hegemony of the Roman liturgical understandings of the day, that is, except for the inconvenient work of Dr. Olson, who persuaded the three participating churches to have a conference to consider the issues involved in restoring the eucharistic prayer without the clear Lutheran option of only the words of institution. The seriousness of the issues at stake was not widely understood.

> **Traditional Lutherans could not make an argument against these practices, given the hegemony of the Roman liturgical understandings of the day ... except for the inconvenient work of Dr. Olson, who persuaded the three participating churches to have a conference to consider the issues involved ...**

In a poll, pastors in the ALC had overwhelmingly approved the eucharistic prayer despite the fact that their teachers, especially Gerhard Forde, of Luther Seminary opposed it.

> **Olson succeeded against all odds. ... The gathered group, including such Lutheran luminaries as Arthur Carl Piepkorn, Missouri's grand old man, could not defeat Olson's historical arguments and logic.**

Olson succeeded against all odds. A Theological Symposium on the Liturgy met on October 3-5, 1974, in Waukegan, Illinois. The gathered group, including such Lutheran luminaries as Arthur Carl Piepkorn, Missouri's grand old man, could not defeat Olson's historical arguments and logic. They knew his argument was incontrovertible on historical and theological grounds, no matter how much they disliked it. One worthy, according to Olson, even burst into tears when he saw what was at stake.

The *Lutheran Book of Worship* (*LBW*) committee was thus compelled to include the bare verba—just the words of institution—in addition to its preferred eucharistic prayer.

The result was that the *LBW* included the following three rubrics which, unfortunately, are presented as options of equal standing:

Rubric 31: The old Hippolytan eucharistic prayer (*LBW*, 69, 89, 110), which Olson opposed.

Rubric 32: The bare verba, which is the only form that Luther considered appropriate for evangelical worship (*LBW*, 69, 89, 110).

Rubric 33: This was a compromise suggested by Olson with an *Amen* after the Prayer of Thanksgiving that concluded the upward direction of the prayer before the words of institution directed to the people, or down (*LBW*, 70, 90, 111).

Olson Regarded as Pariah

For his efforts Olson came to be regarded as a pariah in the church and did not receive tenure at St. Olaf College, Luther Seminary, or finally Philadelphia Seminary, despite his excellent reputation as a controversial but great teacher. One of the most learned students of the liturgy in his time, Oliver was unique among Lutheran scholars. Few had the intellectual heft and historical awareness to teach students how to consider theologically liturgical traditions and innovations. His work combined the theological, historical, musical, aesthetical, and congregational expertise necessary for the pastor who would plan truly evangelical services for his or her congregations. Sadly, because of opposition to his ideas, he found no Lutheran school where he could stay and teach what he knew to upcoming Lutheran pastors.

LBW and Worship Wars

With the introduction of the *LBW* in 1978 Lutheran worship entered conflicted times. The Lutheran worship establishment at the time had imbibed a very different notion of what the morning service was to do. The music of the *LBW* liturgy settings was modern, an alien sound for most Americans who have consistently shunned the concert halls when modern music is played. Furthermore, the addition of many venerable old Lutheran chorales from the age of Lutheran orthodoxy, included to please the Missouri Synod that by 1976 had withdrawn from the project, made the book a strange anomaly to many young pastors. Those beginning their ministries in the 1980s often abandoned it because it didn't feel right to them. If the *LBW* was traditional Lutheran worship they wanted nothing to do with traditional Lutheran worship—they did not deem it helpful in making new Christians, something they were desperate to do, given their warm evangelical interests.

What they rejected, however, was not traditional Lutheran worship. A Lutheran liturgy eschewing the work of Martin Luther, based on the findings of Vatican II, and set to difficult modern music could hardly be called "traditional."

As contemporary worship gained dominance in Lutheran churches interested in growth, many of the pastors and musicians did not conceive of themselves as traditional at all. In some strange almost instinctual way, they were. Until this time Lutheran worship had understood itself to be public, open to all comers, including the seekers and inquirers.

His work combined the theological, historical, musical, aesthetical, and congregational expertise necessary for the pastor who would plan truly evangelical services for his or her congregations.

Until this time Lutheran worship had understood itself to be public, open to all comers, including the seekers and inquirers.

Liturgy: Work of the People?

Lutheran worship, however, had changed: Now worship leaders taught their people that liturgy was the "work of the people," not God's. Worship was play, some theologians argued, a drama in which we were the actors and God was the audience. The result of this was the conclusion that worship could only be for Christians.

Luther had, however, been very clear in his introduction to the *Deutsche Messe* that the service was a time to "make" Christians (Matt. 28.19), when non-Christians could actually be converted. Luther's idea that church should be where we came to hear God's word receded in favor of liturgy as the work of the people. Not surprisingly the worship wars broke out; ignorant armies clashed in a wearisome conflict about music, but on another level about evangelism. Lutherans were bewildered by this split and came to find that Sunday worship no longer refreshed them with the proclamation of the word, but wearied them because now it was their work.

Lutheran Emphasis: Confessional or Liturgical?

When the Evangelical Lutheran Church in America (ELCA) was formed and the young church began to prepare for a new book of worship that would become *Evangelical Lutheran Worship* (*ELW*) and the development of all the resources with which we are now inundated, the group planning it made little reference to Oliver's work.

It helps to understand certain developments leading to this situation in the ELCA: Whereas the *Service Book and Hymnal* had one version of the eucharistic prayer (the "Prayer of Thanksgiving," *SBH*, 34, 62), *Lutheran Book of Worship* also had only one (rubric 31, *LBW*, 69, 89, 110). But, unlike the *SBH*, which included the bare verba on pages 35 and 63 (i.e., just the words of institution, which are based only on Scripture), *LBW* included the bare verba as an option (rubric 32, *LBW*, 69, 89, 110) but only after much scholarly debate and outcry—which was initiated, in large part, by Oliver Olson.

A telling characteristic of *Evangelical Lutheran Worship* is that it offers ten versions of the eucharistic prayer: versions I, III, IV (*ELW*, 108, 110, 111) and versions V through XI, (*ELW*, 65-70), where they are labeled "Thanksgiving at the Table."

It was only after much protest, however, during the development phase, that the ELCA's hymnal committee relented and included the *only* proper form for which Luther advocated—the bare verba—offered as option II (*ELW*, 108, 130). Still, the feel of the Lutheran service has changed. Unfortunately, most Lutherans are no longer defining themselves as "confessional," but "liturgical."

Reclaiming Evangelical Worship

As the new worship book in the ELCA came to completion, we at ReClaim asked Olson to write a book that would explain these issues to an audience of pastors, seminary students, interested laity, and theologians. They need to have a theologically sound Lutheran set of principles guiding them as they lead worship that is truly evangelical and refreshing to contemporary people.

What you hold in your hand is the result of that urging, but also something that is in its way a first, at least in our day—a book about Lutheran liturgical practices seen in the light of Lutheran theology by a learned scholar who loves and values the insights of the Reformation, especially Matthias Flacius.

Oliver's book should be the beginning of a new liturgical revival among Lutherans interested in furthering the insights of Martin Luther in the future. If we are to grow as a movement, we will need wise and flexible pastors and laity who are able to discern what is necessary for truly evangelical worship in their own contemporary congregations.

> **What you hold in your hand is ... a book about Lutheran liturgical practices seen in the light of Lutheran theology ...**

Chapter 1

Christ's Command: "Do This"

God's Initiative

The history of ritual is largely a history of what *humans* do. But Luther insisted that in the liturgy *God* does something. The Christian mass, he insisted, bucking a long history, activates God's testament, his last will. Students of the liturgy should read the masterful treatments of "testament" by Kenneth Hagen.[1] Martin Luther's authority was Hebrews 9.17, "For a will takes effect only at death, since it is not in force as long as the one who made it is alive."

> Who has ever heard that he who receives an inheritance has done a good work? He simply takes for himself a benefit. Likewise in the mass we give nothing to Christ, but only receive from him; unless they are willing to call this a good work, that a person sits still and permits himself to be benefited, given food and drink, clothed and healed, helped and redeemed.[2]

As liturgical reformer, Luther ranks with Pope Gregory the Great (ca. 540–604). The liturgy was too long, so Gregory shortened it. The words *kyrie eleison* sung alone, to cite one example, were originally a response in a litany. But Luther's reform is more interesting than Gregory's because he solved a more interesting problem—*how to reform the liturgy that had come to be understood as a sacrifice*. Because today his reform is under attack even in churches called "evangelical Lutheran," it is time to take stock of our evangelical heritage.

1 Kenneth Hagen, "From Testament to Covenant," Sixteenth Century Journal III (1972): 13. Idem. *A Theology of Testament in the Young Luther: The Lectures on Hebrews* (Leiden: E.J. Brill, 1974).

2 E. Theodore Bachman and Helmut T. Lehman, eds., *Luther's Works*, vol. 35 (Philadelphia: Muhlenberg Press, 1960), 93 [hereafter cited as LW].

As liturgical reformer, Luther ranks with Pope Gregory the Great …

Since the Reformation, the church's ancient forms again are vehicles not for sacrifice, but for receiving God's gifts. Modern Swedish theologian Ragnar Bring backs Luther.

> The sacrament, then, is a gift of God. If the gospel is to be expressed through the sacraments, we must wholeheartedly adopt the conception of God as giver. If there is the slightest thought that the communion is an offering to God, a sacred act in God's direction, then the gospel is rendered null and void at once.[3]

Confessional Authority

Wisely, at the Reformation our churches did not adopt a uniform liturgy. Instead, they adopted a *standard*, Jesus' liturgical command "Do this." Since that command appears no less than four times in the New Testament, there is no doubt that he really said it. His mandate therefore must govern the church's practice. To clarify exactly what Jesus commanded and to identify abuses that had blemished the liturgy, Lutheran Reformers agreed on the "Nihil Rule." It was approved by Martin Luther, Philipp Melanchthon, and Martin Bucer in the Wittenberg Concord of 1535 and made official in 1577 in the Formula of Concord.

The Nihil Rule: No Sacrament Outside the Use

Nothing (*nihil*) has the character of a sacrament apart from the use instituted by Christ, or apart from the divinely instituted action. (That is, if Christ's institution is not observed as he established it, there is no sacrament.) This rule dare not be rejected in any way, but it can and should be followed and preserved in the church of God with great benefit.[4]

Bread-Breaking: A Utilitarian Matter

According to the *Nihil Rule*, obedience to Jesus' command "Do this" means consecrate, distribute, receive, eat, and drink.[5] *But not break.*[6]

---

3 "On the Lutheran Concept of the Sacrament," *World Lutheranism of Today: A Tribute to Anders Nygren*, 15 November 1950 (Rock Island, Illinois, 1950), 87.

4 Formula of Concord, Solid Declaration, Article VII:85. Robert Kolb and Timothy J. Wengert, eds., *The Book of Concord: The Confessions of the Evangelical Lutheran Church* (Minneapolis: Fortress Press, 2000), 608 [hereafter cited as BC].

5 Ibid.

6 Johann Gerhard, "Argumentum contra repraesentativam fractionem IV," *Loci Communes Theologici 9* (Tübingen, 1967): 283; Oliver K. Olson, "The 'Fractio Panis' in Heidelberg and Antwerp," Derk Visser, ed., *Controversy and Conciliation: The Reformation and the Palatinate 1559–1583* [Pittsburg Theological Monographs, New Series 18] (Allison Park, Penn: Pickwick Publications, 1986), 147-153; Bodo Nischan, "The 'Fractio Panis,' A Reformed Communion Practice in Late Reformation Germany," *Church History* 53 (1984): 17-29.

Chapter 1 • Christ's Command: "Do This"

Weighing *exactly* what Jesus meant, our classic theologians distinguished *formal* acts from *concomitant* acts. They were following Luther's distinction between *Thaetell-Worte* ("He gave thanks. He broke. He gave. He said.") and the *Heisel-Wort* of Christ himself ("Take, eat; this do …"), which, Luther explained, meant eat and drink.[7]

For two centuries after the Reformation that careful distinction was a central matter, and whoever is interested in fidelity to the Lutheran heritage should know about the controversy. Some groups, for instance, were insisting "This do" meant that communion was valid only when taken as the apostles did, in groups of twelve. Other concomitant acts could be renting a private house with an upper room, reclining, eating roast lamb, and serving only "one loaf" (1 Corinthians 10.7). But these other things are unnecessary for a valid sacrament. They are *concomitant* acts.

In practice, the controversy about concomitant acts settled down to one act—whether to break the bread. For two centuries, the Lutherans insisted that breaking bread (the *fraction*) is not a formal act, but a concomitant act. It is merely utilitarian, fitting large bread into small mouths. Think: brittle pita bread. (Tearing up a normal, soft American bread loaf, of course, has no similarity to the practice at the Last Supper.)

One of our famous orthodox theologians, Johannes Quenstedt, wrote:
> It is permissible that the bread be broken in connection with the distribution. Nevertheless, it is not one of the formal acts of the sacrament, nor is it necessary that the fraction take place during the celebration. It is an arbitrary matter and can be taken care of before the Holy Supper.[8]

In 1707 theologian David Hollatz, wrote:
> What Christ commanded is clear from the words of institution, "Take, eat, this is my body, this do in remembrance of me." Here there is no mention of the fraction … the fraction of the bread [Latin: *fractio panis*] at the first supper was an accidence, done because the bread was very large, and, as is usual among Hebrews, fragile.[9]

According to the Late Reformation Confession of Antwerp of 1567:
> "This do" refers only to the preceding command to accept and eat the bread and wine, the body and blood of the Lord, and reciting the

---

7 Christoph Pelargus in *Sammlung von Alten und Neuen* (1724): 186f.

8 *Theologia Didacto-polemica,* (Wittenberg, 1710): IV 216.

9 *Examen theologicum acromaticum universam theologiam thetico-polemicam complectens* (Leipzig and Rostock, 1707): 607.

words of Christ. And not to everything preceeding, to the circumstances, which are not essential things commanded by Christ, but are clearly free matters.[10]

In 1965 German theologian Hans-Joachim Kraus wrote:

> … already the old expression, "breaking of bread," shows that there is no question here of a cultic meal in the sense of a "sacred supper." The adoption of Jewish usages contributed to the exclusion from the early Lord's Supper of any cultic significance.[11]

Disregarding fears about the spread of germs, some today also insist on using "one cup." Many are sensibly reluctant to drink from the same cup used by dozens; others are distracted from thoughts about communion with God to worries about sanitation. It is important to realize that while drinking is a formal matter, the use of "one cup" is a concomitant matter. A good jeweler can fashion a pouring spout for the chalice and eliminate distraction.

[10] *Confessio Ministrorum Jesu Christi, in Ecclesia Antverpiensi, quae Augustanae Confessioni adsentitur*, n.p. (1567): Kvv.

[11] "Gottesdienst im alten und im neuen Bund," *Evangelische Theologie* 25 (1965): 199f.

A small cup is one option to the unsanitary common cup; a "shot glass" is not the only alternative.

Bread-Breaking: Luther vs Melanchthon

The fraction of the bread is not an important matter for most people, but making fine distinctions is the responsibility of theologians. The question about whether to break the bread leads to the need *to distinguish between imitation and obedience.*

Chapter 1 • Christ's Command: "Do This"

For Luther, the real presence of Christ was bound up with the question of consecration. Fellow Reformer Philipp Melanchthon disagreed. Rather than by means of consecration, he argued, the presence was brought about by the human *use*.[12] He misused 1 Corinthians 10.16.

> "The bread which we break is it not a participation (*koinonia*) in the body of Christ?" … [Paul] does not say that the nature of the bread is changed, as the papists say. He does not say, like the men in Bremen, that the bread is the substantial body of Christ. He does not say, like Heshusius [and Luther], that the bread is the true body of Christ. But he says it is the *koinonia*, that is, the thing by which it becomes consociated with the body of Christ.[13]

"Melanchthon's fall from this [Lutheran] doctrine," wrote German and Australian theologian, Hermann Sasse, "is based on his transfer of the real presence from the elements to [emphasis on] the sacramental action."[14]

"Whoever proceeds from action," wrote Helmut Gollwitzer, "thereby already stands outside of the real Lutheran doctrine of the sacrament; that goes for everyone from Melanchthon to Althaus."[15] His defection was important in his becoming the "father of Reformed theology."[16]

Melanchthon's notion was adopted in question 75 of the Heidelberg catechism of the German Reformed Church.

> **Question:** How are you reminded and assured in the Holy Supper that you participate in the one sacrifice of Christ on the cross and in all his benefits?
>
> **Answer:** In this way: Christ has commanded me and all believers to eat of *this broken bread,* and to drink of this cup in remembrance of him. He has thereby promised that his body was offered and *broken on the cross* for me, and that his blood was shed for me, as surely as I see him with my eyes that *the bread of the Lord is broken for me,* and the cup is shared with me.

The *Little Book on Bread-Breaking,* published officially, concurrent with the Heidelberg Catechism, required (1) a visual action, and (2) ritual imitation.[17] Agreeing, the Calvinist Synod of Wesel decided that breaking was *absolutely necessary.*[18]

> We hold that the fraction is absolutely necessary because it was obviously instituted by Christ and has been practiced by the apostles and

---

12 *Corpus Reformatorum* (Berlin et al., 1834), 4:249 [hereafter CR].

13 Ibid. 9:962.

14 *Was heist lutherisch?* (Munich: C. Kaiser, 1934), 153.

15 *Coena Domini* (Munich: Chr. Kaiser, 1937), 34.

16 Heinrich Heppe with Ernst Bizer, *Die Dogmatik der evangelische-reformierten Kirche* (Neukirchen: Neukirchener Verlag, 1958), xii.

17 *Erzelung Etlicher ursachen, warumb das hochwirdige Sacrament des Nachtmals unsers Herrn und Heylandts Jhesu Christi nicht sole ohne das brotbrechen gehalten werden* (Heidelberg, 1563, 1565), D iij.

18 Oliver Olson, "The Liturgy and Concomitant Aspects of the Lord's Supper," J. Bart Day et al, eds., *Lord Jesus Christ, Will You Not Stay: Essays in Honor of Ronald Feuerhahn on the Occasion of His Sixty-Fifth Birthday* (Houston, Texas: The Feuerhahn Festschrift Committee, 2002), 123.

the whole of the ancient church, and not without very weighty reasons.[19]

Bread-breaking, moreover, was one of the four "Points for Improvement" (*Verbesserungspunkte*) by which Lutheran churches in Germany became Calvinist churches, and at the formation of the Prussian Union was the ceremony by which pastors officially renounced the Augsburg Confession (1530).

Bread-Breaking: Symbol of Nothing

In the eleventh and twelfth centuries, liturgical reform put an end to breaking bread during the service—a task that had become tedious. Thereafter, bread for church was baked bite-size. But priests were still directed to break the bread—just one piece—apparently for the sake of symbolism.

Lutheran critics, however, insisted that *the fraction symbolizes nothing at all*. Certainly not Christ's broken body! Saint John (19.36) reports that "not a bone was broken." Since it was perceived as unnecessary, it was generally abandoned. One Lutheran order of 1552 reads:

> Some take a large particle [that is, the priest's bread], break it apart and hold it up with both hands. Such a custom ought to be abolished because it is just as aggravating as the elevation itself.[20]

Obedience versus Imitation

The dominant figure during the activity leading up to the 1978 *Lutheran Book of Worship* was an Anglican monk, Gregory Dix, who influenced American Lutherans with his book called *The Shape of the Liturgy*. Dix argued that the liturgy is an *imitation* of the Last Supper. He wrote that we must imitate Jesus' four actions: taking, blessing, *breaking*, and eating.[21] (Imitating a primeval event is common to pagan religions.)

Dix convinced almost all our liturgical leaders, both in the Missouri Synod and the church bodies then in the process of uniting in the Evangelical Lutheran Church in America (ELCA). Missouri Synod Pastor Herbert F. Lindemann reported that Jesus' command "involves the fourfold action of taking (offertory), blessing (consecration), *breaking*

---

19 Albrecht Wolters, *Reformationsgeschichte der Stadt Wesel* (Bonn: Adolph Marcus, 1868), 351.

20 "Kirchen-Ordnung Heinricus IV von 30. August 1552," Emil Sehling, *Die evangelischen Kirchenordnungen des XVI, Jahrhunderts* I/II (Aalen: Scientia Verlg, 1970), 154.

21 Gregory Dix, *The Shape of the Liturgy* (Westminster: Dacre Press, 1945), xi. 48. The "four-action shape" has become almost a basic doctrine of Anglicanism. Bernhard Lohse, *A Short History of Christian Doctrine*, (Philadephia: Fortress Press, 1953), 20f.

Chapter 1 • Christ's Command: "Do This"

(fraction), and giving (sharing—the distribution)."[22] Dix's *shape* also appeared as the skeleton of the Missouri Synod's trial order, the *Worship Supplement*.[23]

The rationale of the "four-action shape," wrote ELCA theologian Robert Jenson, was "exactly like" that of the Formula of Concord.[24] Not so. Whereas the Nihil Rule requires *obedience*, the "four-action shape" requires *imitation*. Here, a confessional principle is at stake.

As if the Nihil Rule did not exist, the 1970–1972 International Anglican-Lutheran Conversation reported that "In the Lord's Supper the church obediently performs the acts commanded by Christ, who took bread and wine, gave thanks, broke the bread, and distributed the bread and wine."[25] The "four-action shape" was the structure also of *Contemporary Worship*, the preliminary publication leading to *Lutheran Book of Worship*. Also, according to American Lutheran Church (ALC, a predecessor body of the ELCA) Pastor Mandus Egge, too, *we must imitate the Last Supper*. "In the celebration of the Eucharist there are four basic actions," he wrote. "These *remain unchangeable for they were the actions of Jesus in instituting the sacrament*."[26] Luther Reed, a prominent Lutheran liturgical leader, recommended "a blessing or thanksgiving which includes four actions in imitation of our Lord's actions at the Last Supper."[27]

From the two-hundred-year-long controversy between Lutherans and Calvinists about breaking of bread, it became clear that there are two attitudes about the order for communion. It is either (1) obedience to Christ's command, or (2) imitation of the Last Supper. When they properly understand their own tradition, Lutheran theologians teach *obedience*. According to Luther:

> Therefore we will admit no example, not even from Christ himself, much less from other saints, for it must also be accompanied by God's Word, which explains to us in what sense we are to follow or not to follow it.[28]

The "four-action shape" has now been largely abandoned, along with the dated argument of Eugene Brand, editor of *Lutheran Book of Worship*:

When they properly understand their own tradition, Lutheran theologians teach *obedience*.

22 Herbert Fred Lindeman, *The New Mood in Lutheran Worship* (Minneapolis: Augsburg, 1971), 53f.
23 *Worship Supplement* (St. Louis: Concordia, 1969), 59-62.
24 "A Great Thanksgiving for Lutherans?" *Response* XV (1975): 56.
25 *Lutheran World* XIX (1972): 393.
26 "Let There Be Surprise," *Journal of Church Music*, 13 (1971): 5.
27 Luther D. Reed, *The Lutheran Liturgy*, rev. ed. (Philadelphia: Fortress Press, 1947), 355.
28 LW 40:132.

"This four-fold shape is essential to the sacrament. *Leave out any part and you will have no grounds to call what has been done the Lord's Supper.*"[29] According to that logic, for the last five centuries the Sacrament of the Altar in evangelical Lutheran churches (in which bread was not broken) has been invalid.

Re-Enacted Ritual?

The distinction between *obedience* and *imitation* remains more important today than ever, since the urge for imitating apparently never goes away. According to Mark Chapman, a spokesman for the powerful new movement called "Evangelical–Catholic," the Lord's Supper is *imitation*, a "re-enacted ritual."[30]

Martin Luther opposed the notion that salvation is earned by something we do. He also opposed the notion that Holy Communion is something we do. His insight, of course, requires careful thought, since Jesus himself commanded us to do something. So the question has to be asked, what is more important, his words "This do," or his other words "For you"? Careful thought about what our Lord wanted four hundred years ago led to the Nihil Rule, an appropriate place to begin our investigation.

---

[29] "Ceremonial Forms and Contemporary Life," *Response* VIII (1966).

[30] "Fundamental Unity. Evangelical-Catholic Non-Negotiables," *Lutheran Forum*, Christmass [sic] (2005): 13.

Chapter 1 • Christ's Command: "Do This"

For Discussion

1. At various times Christians have served honey, milk, water, grape juice at communion—in America even Coca-Cola. According to the simple sense of the command "This do," what is right?

2. Does the alcohol in communion wine prevent contamination?

3. What theological point is involved in the question whether to break the bread or not?

4. Is the Nihil Rule still reliable after 400 years?

Participants may consult the Nihil Rule in the Book of Concord (see the Formula of Concord, Solid Declaration, Article VII, 85:608).

Chapter 2

Liturgical Novelties

Through the centuries, liturgical changes were made. The boldest alteration of the communion service dates from 1215 A.D. Combining pagan notions of the philosopher Aristotle with Christian teaching, the Fourth Lateran Council defined consecrating bread and wine "transubstantiation." Altar bread, then, became Christ's body *permanently*.

Reservation of the "Host"

Meanwhile, the permanently transubstantiated bread was "reserved," that is, stored in a *sacrament house*, a *tabernacle*, or *aumbry*. The word *host* means "sacrifice" and therefore is not appropriate for Lutheran churches. Nor does a red sanctuary light, the signal that the bread was reserved, make sense. Luther's advice:

> Since the use of the Holy Eucharist is participation in it, and communion of the faithful in remembrance of Christ, it is not to be reserved in chests or in aumbries in any way or in any place.[31]

Rather than "reservation" in a depositing-place on the way to the hospital or sickbed, evangelical Lutheran practice is a complete consecration for each communicant.

> In houses where there are sick people, the words of the Lord Christ, with which He instituted the Holy Sacrament, shall be spoken with a loud voice over the bread and wine, so that the sick and other people who are present understand what is being done; we have no command

31 Edward Frederick Peters, "The Origin and Meaning of the Axiom, 'Nothing Has the Character of a Sacrament Outside the Use in Sixteenth-Century and Seventeenth-Century Lutheran Theology,'" Doctoral Dissertation (St. Louis: Concordia Seminary, 1968), 306.

> **Rather than "reservation" in a depositing-place on the way to the hospital or sickbed, evangelical Lutheran practice is a complete consecration for each communicant.**

from Christ to reserve the sacrament in the monstrance and to carry it around or to go with the sacrament to the sick.[32]

The sacrament is not to be reserved, but is to be consecrated before the sick person; therefore the minister is to take the bread and wine so that the sick person may hear the salutary words.

> The sacrament shall no longer be given to the sick without the Word and command of our Lord Jesus Christ, because it is clear that we should not have such a sacrament without the Word; therefore the consecration shall take place in the presence of the sick person, so that he can hear it, and also receive the sacrament in both kinds.[33]

Thoughtful pastors may also invite others present to take part.

Corpus Christi Procession

About 1264 Pope Urban IV made the first Thursday after Trinity Sunday the festival of Corpus Christi, and the altar bread was paraded through the streets. But Luther advised the church to abandon sacrament houses and the Corpus Christi processions, because "there is no need for them."[34] Church orders followed him, for example, in the city of Homberg:

> There is no doubt that the papistic adoration in procession, in reservation, and in the oblation is simply idolatrous because nothing has the character of a sacrament outside of the use instituted by God, since no creature can make a Sacrament.[35]

The thirteenth-century doctrinal blunder was corrected at the Reformation. Christ is present bodily during the *use* of the sacrament, *but not afterwards.*

How Long Does the Presence Last?

According to some theologians, we should not ask such questions, but curious Lutherans have often asked them anyway. About 1555 the Erfurt theologian John Hachenburg wrote:

> It is not within our power to proclaim according to our own understanding or thoughts when the Sacraments begin and when they cease and end, but rather one must judge by the Word of God, and let what it says prevail. Now the Word says that Christ took bread and wine

---

32 Ibid., 315.
33 Ibid., 316.
34 LW 36:291.
35 CR 9:276.

into His hands and spoke these words over them: "This is my Body. This is my Blood." And from that hour on, that is what they are. For what He commands and says—that happens and is there. As Psalm 33 [9] says: "He spoke and it came to be: he commanded, and it stood forth."[36]

If one does insist on asking how long the presence lasts, the answer is: about from the beginning of the Lord's Prayer until all have communed, the chalice has been emptied, the bread has been consumed, the people dismissed, and [the pastor] has left the altar.[37]

Visual Communion

For the sake of visibility, in the Middle Ages the altar bread was raised above the head of the priest. Originally, Luther favored the practice, since it was not clear exactly what it meant. But the *elevation* gradually disappeared in evangelical churches.

In the ceremony of *ostensio*, just before distribution, priests used to invite people to *gaze* at the bread.[38] For visibility the bread was framed in an *ostensorium* or *monstrance*. The notion of adoration led to the "benediction of the blessed sacrament," a ceremony that involves *looking*. In some places that visual communion was expanded into perpetual adoration with people taking turns at adoring. The communion elements certainly must be held in high honor, but it is clear that Jesus did not say, "This is my body; gaze at it!"

Withholding the Cup

In the Middle Ages it was decided that drinking from the chalice at communion should be limited to priests. Lay persons were given only bread. As the name of the rebels, *calixtine* (from calix, chalice), indicates, the right of lay persons to drink the wine was fiercely fought for in the fifteenth-century Hussite wars in Bohemia. Recently, the Roman Catholic Church changed its mind and now sometimes permits lay persons to drink the wine, but still insists that "withholding the cup" is legitimate. Its doctrine of concomitance is an argument that eating the body logically *includes* drinking blood.

36 Peters, 421.
37 *D. Martin Luthers Werke, Kritische Gesamtausgabe, Weimar,* 1883ff (hereafter WA) *Briefe,* 464.
38 Peters, 286f.

The communion elements certainly must be held in high honor, but it is clear that Jesus did not say, "This is my body; gaze at it!"

But Luther agreed with the Hussites: the biblical accounts should not be modified by philosophical logic, but understood in their simple sense. Obedience to the command, "Take and eat, all of you," could not be cancelled out by talk about concomitance. Theological advisors to the Duke of Saxony argued:

> ... whether both bread and wine should be distributed. That was a question that should not be asked. Christ had already decided the matter.[39]

Intinction

Many congregations find provision for drinking at communion inconvenient, especially when attendance is great or when they are convinced that the Sunday service should not last more than one hour. Some of them resort to the practice of *intinction*. Altar bread is dipped into wine. Intinction has been practiced and defended for a long time. In 1965 the Roman Catholic Church allowed the practice, in spite of the fact that one early pope, Julius I (d. 340), had written against it.

> But their practice of giving the people intincted eucharist for the fulfillment of communion is not received from the gospel witness, where it is recorded that when he gave the apostles his body and blood, giving the bread separately and the chalice separately.[40]

In 1944 the Lutheran Church–Missouri Synod determined that the command, "Drink," is serious.

> We definitely reject intinction because while distributing the bread, the Savior said, "Take, eat!" (Matt. 2.25; Mark 14.11), and while giving the wine, He said, "Drink ye all of it!" (Matt. 25.17; Mark 13.23). Intinction would be a direct violation of the words of institution.[41]

Offertory

Since for a long time gifts to the church were gathered about the same time the sacrament was being prepared, the two actions got confused. The mix resulted in an "offertory" ceremony, whose clear interpretation is that human action matters. In the long history of the liturgy no ceremony has made more mischief.

---

[39] *Der Prediger der Jungen Herrn Johans Friderichen Hertzogen zu Sachssen etc. Söhnten Christlich Bedencken auff das Interim.* n.p. 1548.

[40] *Patrologiae Cursus Completus,* Series Prima, Tomus VIII (Paris: Vrayet, 1844), 970.

[41] *Proceedings of the 1944 Saginaw, Michigan, Convention,* 254f.

The offertory ritual played a great part in the development of the misleading doctrine, the "sacrifice of the mass." For a long time the prayer over the collection even had an official name, "minor canon," second in importance to the mass canon (eucharistic prayer). There is no clearer example of the ancient dictum *lex orandi lex credendi* (the law of prayer is the law of believing).

Roman Catholic Theodor Klauser observed that the offertory procession has its roots in the sacrificial rituals of pagan ceremonies.[42] A fellow liturgical expert, Joseph Jungmann, wrote that preparation for communion need not be a ceremony.

> The preparation of bread and wine does not yet need to be a ritual act. It can also be taken care of before the beginning of the celebration itself by someone or other. In the most ancient accounts we sense nothing of a special emphasis on the action of preparation. As long as the eucharist was connected with the fraternal meal, there was no need for it. The gifts were already on the table..[43]

According to the 1937 Faith and Order Conference, an early ecumenical movement, "The Holy Communion is not possible without the offering."[44] But the command, "Do this," does not include an offertory. A better practice is to collect tithes and gifts simply, without ceremony, during a hymn.[45] Thus, the liturgical focus can be kept as it should be—not on our works, but on God's grace.

At one point the procession was curtailed. Altar boys carried the communion elements, but only for a few feet, from the "credence table" to the altar. But since Vatican Council II (1962–1965) the procession has been stretched out again, and begins at the front door. Lay persons carry bread and wine together with collected money to the altar. The meaning of the procession is self-sacrifice. When the elements are consecrated by the priests, the believers' self-sacrifice, so the argument goes, is united with Christ's sacrifice on Calvary. Despite the doubtful significance, the new hymnal *Evangelical Lutheran Worship* authorizes the eucharistic procession: "… bread and wine may be brought forward" (*ELW,* 128, 144, etc.).

> **… the command, "Do this," does not include an offertory.**

42 *A Short History of the Western Liturgy* (London: Oxford, 1969), 9.

43 *Missarum Sollemnia* II (Vienna, Freiburg, Basel: Herder, 1962), 3.

44 *The Second World Conference on Faith and Order Held at Edinburgh August 3-18, 1937* (New York: MacMillan, 1938), 328.

45 *ReClaim, Introductory Edition: Lutheran Hymnal for Church and Home* (Minneapolis: Bronze Bow Publishing, 2006), 26.

For Discussion

1. Why is there no wine in a Corpus Christi procession?

2. What right does a sick person have when a pastor brings communion?

3. Is intinction a valid response to the command, "Do this"?

4. How much time of the Sunday service does the practice of intinction save? How important is the time saved?

5. What is the intrinsic meaning of a eucharistic procession?

Chapter 3

The Lord's Supper

In his reform of the liturgy, Luther carefully followed Jesus' words, "Do this," and eliminated the liturgical novelties.

> You are not to choose or designate either your own words or your own element, and you are to do nothing at all or permit anything to be done that is of your own invention, but rather it is His command and order that establishes for you both word and element and this you should keep without any change whatever.[46]

Since Jesus' words have nothing to do with sacrifice, the reformed order can no longer be called the church's supper. It is the Lord's Supper. Luther's advice was repeated in the Formula of Concord.

> … we must accept the words [of institution] as they stand, in their proper, clear sense, with simple faith and appropriate obedience and not permit ourselves to be drawn away from this position by any objection or human counter-argument spun out of human reason, no matter how attractive it may appear to our human reason.[47]

Luther's Historical Judgment

Practitioners of the biblical historical-critical method have sometimes cast doubt on anchoring the liturgy in the biblical account. But because the words of institution are quoted four times in the New Testament they are doubtlessly authentic, and there is no doubt that their context was a ritual *and that they are an instruction for the church* (1 Cor. 11.23-26; Matt. 26.26-29; Mark 14.22-25; Luke 22.14-20).

46 Peters, 132.
47 Formula of Concord, Solid Declaration, Article VII:45 [BC].

Words of institution … four times … 1 Cor. 11.23-26; Matt. 26.26-29; Mark 14.22-25; Luke 22.14-20.

Although some early Calvinists opted for other words, today there is general agreement that the words of institution should be used. *The contemporary controversy is about whether additional human words are necessary.*

According to compilers of *Evangelical Lutheran Worship*, human words *are* necessary.

> **Principle 43:** The biblical words of institution declare God's action and invitation. They are set within the context of the Great Thanksgiving. This eucharistic prayer proclaims and celebrates the gracious work of God in creation, redemption, and sanctification.[48]

"But it is important for the understanding of the whole future history of the liturgy," wrote Gregory Dix, "to grasp the fact that *eucharistic worship from the outset was not based on Scripture at all*, whether of the Old or New Testament, but solely on tradition."[49]

For Lutherans, only the New Testament accounts are the norm. But for Roman Catholics the norm is liturgy of the fourth century. The editors of the 1978 *Lutheran Book of Worship* shared the Roman Catholic notion. Reporting about the controversy thirty years ago, William Rusch, ELCA ecumenical officer, wrote:

> One side of the argument has viewed the proposals of the commission [the Inter-Lutheran Commission on Worship] as a betrayal of the fundamentals of the Reformation and has regarded the sixteenth century as normative. The other side of the discussion [within the ILCW] has seen the work of the commission as moving beyond the consensus of the sixteenth century, solving problems the reformers could not, and has considered the early church, especially the fourth century, as normative.[50]

The difficulty with fourth-century authority is that we do not know much about the liturgy of the first three centuries. "In the restoration of the eucharistic prayer," Luther Reed wrote, "*we return to the earlier pre-Roman*

Sidebar — Footnotes:

48 *Renewing Worship, Vol. 2: Principles for Worship* (Augsburg Fortress: Minneapolis, 2002), 134 [hereafter PW].

49 *The Shape of the Liturgy*, (Westminster, England: Dacre Press, 1945), 3 [emphasis original].

50 William G. Rusch, "A Background Paper for a Theological Review of Materials" (Produced by the Inter-Lutheran Commission on Worship, Mimiographed, January, 1977), 34.

Synonyms:

Canon of the mass
Mass canon
Eucharistic prayer
Great Thanksgiving
The Prayer of Thanksgiving

conception, according to which the church set apart the elements in a blessing or thanksgiving which includes four actions in imitation of our Lord's actions at the last supper."[51]

But what did Dr. Reed know about the *pre-Roman conception*? How can we *return* to a tradition we know almost nothing about? German theologian Rudolf Stählin reported:

> A clear picture is furnished first by the fourth century, whence the oldest liturgical formulae have been passed down. The decisive question, with which that fact confronts us, is this: Are the liturgies of the fourth century the direct development and the organic unfolding of the rudiments given in the New Testament, or is there a breach between the two periods? Is there continuity, or do we have to judge that the original was falsified in a "catholic" manner?[52]

Roman Catholics *assume* that in the second and third centuries the liturgy remained faithful—in spite of the heresies plaguing the church in other ways. But the "falsification" Stählin thought possible did not take place just because improvised human words (at first, free prayers) were mixed with the words of institution. Those "human words" had no effect on doctrine as long as they were improvised.

At first, they were "simply a Christian version of the grace after the meal."[53] They became a source of doctrine first *when they were congealed*. The final stage of a long development, when "human words" were decreed *necessary* for the consecration, was the Council of Trent (1545–1563).

Luther called the extra words "human productions, additions to the words of Christ, things without which the mass would still continue, and remain at its best."[54]

Aware of the lack of evidence from the early history of the liturgy, Luther responsibly concluded that the only reliable evidence of liturgical forms in the time of the apostles and after is the New Testament itself.

> On them [the words of institution] we must rest. On them we must build as on a firm rock if we would not be carried about with every wind of doctrine ... For in these words nothing is omitted that pertains to the completeness, the use, and the blessing of the sacraments.[55]

---

[51] Luther D. Reed, *The Lutheran Liturgy*, rev. ed. (Philadelphia: Fortress Press, 1947), 355 [emphasis added].

[52] Rudolf Stählin, "Die Geschichte des christlichen Gottesdienstes von der Urkirche bis zur Gegenwart," *Leiturgia: Handbuch des Evangelischen Gottesdienstes. I.* (Kassel: Johannes Stauda-Verlag, 1954), 6.

[53] Joachim Jeremias, *The Eucharistic Words of Jesus* (London: SCM Press, 1966), 117.

[54] *Martin Luther: Selections from His Writings*, John Dillenberger, ed. (New York: Anchor Books, 1961), 271f; LW 36:36.

[55] LW 36:37.

Cyril of Jerusalem (ca. 315–386) narrowed the locus of consecration to the *epiclesis* (invocation of the Holy Spirit) and began the peculiar Eastern tradition of consecration, which conceives of it as a kind of "resurrection" accomplished on a body that has been "killed" in the sacristy. The Western church countered through Saint Augustine (354–430) with the localization of the consecration in the words of institution. The identification of the *verba* (words of institution) as the active agent was continued in the eucharistic controversies of the eighth century and by the two works of Saint Ambrose, *De Sacramentis* and *De Mysteriis*. The highest point of the development came in the teaching of Thomas Aquinas, who taught that the verba alone effect the consecration—with no necessary assistance from the remainder of the canon. We conclude, therefore, that *Luther's judgment about the reliable sources is the authentic liturgical tradition.*

Luther was seconded by German theologian Ferdinand Hahn.

> [The New Testament evidence] must, however, provide a model for renovation and restructuring in the face of all adherence to a later, historically developed form of worship, in the face of all traditionalism and legalism in liturgical matters.[56]

No Human Words!

Against Luther, the Council of Trent insisted that the consecration of the elements be accomplished with a *mix* of divine and human words, "the traditions of the apostles and the pious institutions also of the holy pontiffs."

The committee for *ELW* agrees with the Council of Trent.

> **Principle 43:** The biblical words of institution declare God's action and invitation. They are set within the context of the Great Thanksgiving. This eucharistic prayer proclaims and celebrates the gracious work of God in creation, redemption, and sanctification.[57]

---

56 Ferdinand Hahn, *The Worship of the Early Church* (Philadelphia: Fortress, 1973), 104.

57 PW, 134.

Luther's judgment about the reliable sources is the authentic liturgical tradition.

Chapter 3 • The Lord's Supper

"What is more than the Word," Luther determined, "we should consider against the word of Christ."[58]

> Let us confine ourselves to the very words by which Christ instituted and completed the sacrament and commended it to us. *For these words alone, and apart from everything else, contain the power, the nature and the whole substance of the mass.* All the rest are human productions, additions to the words of Christ, things without which the mass would still continue, and remain at its best.[59]

Setting the words of institution "within the context of the Great Thanksgiving" (*PW*, 134), he wrote, is like imbedding the holy words in a heathen temple.

> From here on [from the offertory] almost everything smacks and savours of sacrifice. *And the words of life and salvation are imbedded in the midst of it all*, just as the ark of the Lord once stood in the idol's temple, next to Dagon … Let us, therefore repudiate everything that smacks of sacrifice, together with the entire canon [eucharistic prayer] and retain only that which "is pure and holy and so order our mass."[60]

But even if the *wording* is altered to erase sacrifice language (which has been tried), the sacrament, Luther wrote, must not be confused with prayer. According to Luther:

> … we must therefore sharply distinguish the testament and sacrament itself from the prayers we offer at the same time.[61]

> Therefore, these two things—mass and prayer, sacrament and work, testament and sacrifice—must not be confused; for the one comes from God to us through the ministration of the priest and demands our faith, the other proceeds from our faith to God through the priest and demands his hearing. The former descends, the latter ascends.[62]

> **Luther:** Give way, canon, give way to the Gospel and give place to the Holy Spirit because you are a human word![63]

His ritual reform was consistent with his theological reform:

> Luther was totally consistent in applying the doctrine of justification

---

… the sacrament, Luther wrote, must not be confused with prayer.

---

58 WA 6:367, 2.
59 *Martin Luther: Selections from His Writings*, John Dillenberger, ed. (New York: Anchor Books, 1916), 271f [emphasis added].
60 LW 53:26.
61 LW 36:50.
62 LW 36:56.
63 WA 8:448.

as the controlling principle to liturgical as well as to all other theological and practical questions: in the Lord's Supper is the offer of forgiveness and grace, and this proclamation of the gospel is enshrined in the *Verba Testamenti* [words of testament, of institution], which are not to be obscured by the addition of humanly-devised tradition, nor confused by making them into a God-directed prayer.[64]

Who would have thought that five centuries later, a church calling itself Lutheran would in its Principle 43 decree that human words are necessary?

Consecrated by Scripture

Following Saint Augustine, Luther taught that the biblical words *consecrate* the bread and wine. "When the Word is joined to the external element," Saint Augustine taught, "it becomes a sacrament."[65] His argument was also Luther's.

> When we say these words over the bread, then he is truly present ... For as soon as Christ says "This is my body" his body is present through the Word and the power of the Holy Spirit. If the Word is not there, it is mere bread; but as soon as the words are added they bring with them that of which they speak.[66]

The Formula of Concord appeals to John Chrysostom (c. 347–407).

> Christ himself prepares this table and blesses it. No human being, but only Christ himself who was crucified for us, can make of the bread and wine set before us the body and blood of Christ. The words are spoken by the mouth of the priest, but by God's power and grace through the words that he speaks, "This is my body," the elements set before us in the Supper are blessed.[67]

Another Consecration

Luther also took for granted that when new elements are brought to the altar during the distribution *another consecration* is necessary.[68] All sixteenth-century theologians recommended it,[69] as did the Common Service of 1888[70] and the *Common Service Book with Hymnal* of 1917.[71] The rubric was omitted in the 1958 *Service Book and Hymnal* (*SBH*). One testimony comes from the 1553 order of the city of Hohenlohe.

> However, wherever hosts or wine run out, he shall have more hosts or wine brought out, and shall again say the Words of Consecration over

---

[64] Robin A. Leaver, "Theological Consistency, Liturgical Integrity, and Musical Hermeneutics in Luther's Liturgical Reforms," *Lutheran Quarterly* 9 (1995): 130f.

[65] Smalcald Articles 5:1 [BC].

[66] LW 36:341.

[67] Formula of Concord, Solid Declaration, Article VII:76 [BC].

[68] Peters, 222, 424.

[69] Ibid., 320.

[70] *The Common Service for the Use of Evangelical Lutheran Congregations*, by authority of the General Synod of the Evangelical Lutheran Church in the United States (Philadelphia: Lutheran Publications Society, 1888).

[71] *Common Service of the Lutheran Church*, authorized by the United Lutheran Church in America (Philadelphia: The Board of Publicaion of the United Lutheran Church in America, 1917).

Receptionism

For centuries some have preferred to adopt *receptionism*. It is an idea pressed by Philipp Melanchthon. Rather than the consecration of bread and wine, which struck him as too Roman Catholic, Melanchthon insisted that Jesus was present only at the moment of reception. The following are receptionist arguments:

> The Lord's Supper is the eating itself, that is, the reception, in which, by the express words of Christ, the body and blood of Christ are conveyed to those who eat, and He is present in those visible things, namely, in bread and wine.[73]

> When [the bread and wine] are consumed, at that time Christ is present and efficacious.[74]

Receptionism has persisted among some Lutherans down to the present, but the Reformation documents collected in the Book of Concord teach consecration of the elements.

Left-Overs: The *Reliquiae*

What, then, after the service, is to be done with the *reliquiae*, the left-overs? There has been a consensus through the years that the remaining elements ought to be handled with respect. Once, centuries ago, it was possible to avoid the problem since everyone was expected to come earlier to confession.

> The priest ... shall prepare the bread and wine on the altar and shall count out as many hosts or particles as the number of communicants that have announced; and shall pour as much wine as he requires into the chalice and set it on the altar.[75]

Luther took it for granted that all of the elements that have been consecrated will be consumed at the same celebration.[76]

> You can do what we do here; you can eat and drink what is left over of the Sacrament with the communicants, so that is not necessary to

---

the bread or wine (whichever has run out); he shall repeat only the Words over the bread or over the chalice.[72]

72 Peters, 320.
73 CR 9:1040.
74 CR 7:876f.
75 Peters, 323.
76 Ibid., 223.

Rather than the consecration of bread and wine, which struck him as too Roman Catholic, Melanchthon insisted that Jesus was present only at the moment of reception.

raise these scandalous and dangerous questions about when the action of the Sacrament cease, questions in which you will be suffocated, unless you come to your senses.[77]

His advice about consuming the elements is still valid. But, since after the *use*, bread and wine are simply bread and wine again, another solution is possible: pouring the wine reverently on the ground, and without ceremony, storing the bread.

Administration, Not Presidency

In a curious way the inter-church movement called "liturgical renewal" has set one Lutheran doctrine against another. In the "renewal vision," the eucharist is *confected* by a priest. Nevertheless, each participant has a "role" in the communal action (*ELW*, 8f). Each role is exercised according to rank. The highest rank is held by the "president," a title invoked in *Principles for Worship* (*PW*, 81). The Lutheran theological tradition, of course, does not use the central term, "president of the eucharist."[78]

On the basis of his (ontological) ordination the priest mistakenly is accorded a special *rank*, and is therefore qualified to serve as president. It is worth mentioning, since it sheds some light on the daily news, that immoral priests have often been favored over victims of sexual abuse because of their rank.

> Accustomed to deferential thinking, today's mismanagers of the clerical scandals do not see themselves as ill-intentioned; ignoring the victims of abuse grows out of the ideology that holds that clergy are different from ordinary people.[79]

Emphasizing the universal priesthood, Martin Luther emphasized that the clergy are no different from ordinary people. He managed to do away with rank in the church. Nevertheless, in the name of universal priesthood, one hears the demand for "lay presidency." The demand is effective in America, because Americans can be expected to rebel against distinctions in rank. We may be tempted to say that pastors are no better than lay persons; therefore, lay persons should be allowed to celebrate communion. Lay persons have *rights*.

---

77 WA *Briefe* 10:341

78 Trevor Lloyd, ed., *Lay Presidency at the Eucharist?* Grove Liturgical Study 9 (Bramcote Notts: Grove Books, 1977).

79 Paul E. Dinter, "A Catholic Crisis, Bestowed from Above," *New York Times*, January 1, 2003.

> In a curious way the inter-church movement called "liturgical renewal" has set one Lutheran doctrine against another.

But universal priesthood does not imply such rights. The difficulty is the notion of "presidency." The Lutheran confessions talk not about *presiding*, but *administering*, which is quite another matter. Resistance to Article XIV as undemocratic misses the point. The Augsburg Confession teaches neither an ontological ordination nor presidency, but the call to public office.

> Concerning church government it is taught that no one should publicly teach, preach, or administer the sacraments without a proper [public] call (Augsburg Confession, Article XIV).

The government, Gerhard Forde observes, that will not allow just any lay person to marry or serve as chaplain, understands "public office" better than do many Christians.[80] The suspicion that assigning "administration" to pastors is undemocratic can be attributed to psychological factors, not to doctrine. All members of the churches are equal, including pastors. Lutheran doctrine is clear that pastors do not have a higher rank. Instead, they have been given a public office, and have different *responsibilities*.

Luther and the confessions restrict preaching and administering the sacraments to those who are called.

> Though we are all equally priests, we cannot all publicly minister and teach. We ought not do so even if we could. Paul writes accordingly in 1 Cor. 4 [1]: "This is how one should regard us, as servants of Christ and stewards of the mysteries of God."[81]

The call to be a *steward* does not have to do with *rank*, but with a special *responsibility*.

> To the extent that, as a "steward of the mysteries of God" he is an administrator of the sacraments, it is in the context of, and as part of, his ministry as a prophetic proclaimer of the Word, the heavenly truth revealed in Jesus Christ.[82]

The responsibility of lay persons in the administration of the sacraments consists in their decision of *whom to call*.

Facing the shortages of priests, Roman Catholics have unfortunately invented "eucharistic ministers," who can distribute altar bread after it has been consecrated by a priest. Here, the emphasis is not on the call, or on

---

Luther and the confessions restrict preaching and administering the sacraments to those who are called.

---

[80] "The Ordained Ministry," Todd Nichol & Mark Kolden, eds., *Called and Ordained: Lutheran Perspectives on the Office of the Ministry* (Minneapolis: Fortress Press, 1990), 126f.

[81] WA 7:58, 19.

[82] Jonathan F. Grothe, "The Mysteries and the Ministry," *Mysteria Dei: Essays in Honor of Kurt Marquart*, Paul T. McCain and John R. Stephenson, eds. (Fort Wayne: Concordia Theological Seminary Press, 1999), 63.

administering, but on the *power to consecrate*. Eucharistic ministers therefore have no place in the Lutheran church.

There is no such thing as "emergency communion." According to Luther, if there is no pastor to administer the sacrament, *Christians should go without communion*. In his letter to the Bohemians he advised private baptism and teaching, but abstention from Holy Communion, since they had no pastors.[83] Luther taught that Holy Communion is not so necessary that salvation depends on it. The believer "can be saved through the word."[84]

About possible "emergency communion," Johann Gerhard (1582–1637) agreed: no argument can be made for lay administration on the basis of necessity.

> [However] never in case of necessity is the administration of the holy supper to be committed to a layman, since in this matter there is a difference from baptism. For Baptism is a Sacrament of initiation but the Holy Supper is a Sacrament of confirmation. Concerning the necessity of baptism, Christ testifies; "unless one shall be born from above in water and Spirit he shall not enter the Kingdom of God." Whenever therefore water is available, Baptism can and ought to be administered by a layman, but there is no use of the holy supper which exists in an equal measure of necessity. Therefore, when there is no supply of ordained ministers of the church, this statement of Augustine holds, "believe and you have eaten."[85]

"The Reformation," according to Ernst Kinder, "did not, as in the Middle Ages, see in the sacraments the chief or even the only media for appropriating God's means of grace in Christ, but rather regarded the sermon as the "chief means of grace."[86]

Not so long ago, lay assistants at communion were rare. Now, almost unnoticed, the practice has become nigh-universal. But because the motto, *lex orandi, lex credendi* is always operative, even partial lay administration unfortunately introduces the notion that as long as the elements are properly consecrated they can be administered by anyone. Thus, Lutheran churches in America are already far advanced in inventing a new doctrine (and of jettisoning Article XIV).

---

83 WA 12:171, 17ff.
84 WA 7 *Briefe* 338.
85 Quoted by William Weinrich, "Should a Layman Discharge the Duties of the Holy Ministry?" Paul T. McCain and John R. Stephenson, *Mysteria Dei: Essays in Honor of Kurt Marquart* (Fort Wayne, Ind. 1999), 349f.
86 "Zur Sakramenstslehre," *Neue Zeitschfit für Systematische Theologie* 3 (1962), 152f.

Luther taught that Holy Communion is not so necessary that salvation depends on it. The believer "can be saved through the word."

Note:
Discussions have raged over the centuries as to what the Latin phrase *rite vocatus* (rightly called or proper call) in the Augsburg Confession, Article 14 means.

Some, like Oliver, argue that it means the pastor of a congregation, who has been called through a churchly process.

Others would say that *rite vocatus* means that a congregation could call a lay person in its midst to fulfill that function in the administering of the sacrament when a pastor is not available.

There is a simple way to *reclaim* Article XIV. Pastors can simply ask someone to help by holding the paten (the bread tray).

Just as rapid: the pastor administers both bread and wine.

The Horror of Historical Absence

As every year distances us further from Jesus' time, many are troubled about discontinuity. Anthony Kemp calls it the "horror of historical absence."[87] One result is that many are attracted to ancient rituals that suggest continuity with the early church. Article VII of the Augsburg Confession is encouraging for those who want "contemporary" worship.

> It is not necessary for the true unity of the Christian church that uniform ceremonies, instituted by human beings, be observed everywhere.

Maintaining Tradition

But rejection of historical forms may contribute to the feeling of that "horror." There is much to be said for retaining ancient ceremonies; they tend to foster a sense of continuity. Helpful at this point may be just one recent observation.

"They want a more traditional understanding of religion and faith," said the Rev. Larry Hollon, general secretary of United Methodist Communications, the marketing and outreach arm of the church.

[87] *The Estrangement of the Past,* (New York: Oxford University Press, 1991), 11.

The contemporary worship that we've come to see in the past couple of decades appeals to the baby boomers, but younger generations connect with a more traditional style of worship ... Quite frankly, that's surprising to us.[88]

As a son of the Western church, Luther favored liturgical continuity and maintaining ancient liturgical treasures. Following his example, the evangelical Lutheran church has inherited the finely-wrought collects constructed on the rigid rules of fourth-century rhetoric; the (post-Gregory) liturgical use of the Nicene Creed, once filed away as just a theological document. We have also inherited the Ordinary of the Mass: the Kyrie Eleison, the Gloria in Excelsis (queen of all Christian hymns), the Sanctus (a marriage of Isaiah's outcry and Jerusalem's shouts to welcome Jesus) and the Agnus Dei. For two hundred years after the Reformation, Lutheran and Roman Catholic churches, common heirs, used each others' composed masses.

"We do not abolish the Mass," echoes the Augsburg Confession, "but religiously keep and defend it."[89] Until the opposition got organized, in fact, much of Europe was convinced that Luther had preserved the pure, ancient, apostolic, *catholic* tradition.

Since congregations are free to assign the singing of the ordinary (Kyrie Eleison, Gloria in Excelsis, Creed, Sanctus, Agnus Dei) to a choir once in a while, contemporary Lutheran churches can certainly make use of those portions of Catholic composed masses.

Luther was traditional also in agreeing with eleventh-century Cardinal Humbert of Silva Candida, who insisted that the Sacrament of the Altar is not trinitarian, but christological.[90] Thus, by upholding the tradition of the Western church, he countered in advance arguments for the prayer of the Eastern Orthodox church (*epiclesis*) for the descent of the Holy Spirit on the bread and wine.

---

88 "Prepare Thee for Serious Marketing," *New York Times*, Oct. 22, 2006.

89 Augsburg Confession, Article XXIV:1 [BC].

90 A. Michel, "Die folgenschweren Ideen des Kardinals Humbert und ihr Einfluss auf Gregor VII": In G. B. Borino, ed., *Studi Gregoriani* I (1947), 65-92.

Chapter 3 • The Lord's Supper

The Common Service: A Near Miracle of Unity

In their chests, immigrants to America brought with them church books and beautiful hymns in the many languages of Europe. But the fond wish of Lutheran patriarch Henry Melchior Muhlenberg was one church book in English.

His wish was realized in the Common Service of 1888. Compiled according to "the common consent of the pure Lutheran liturgies of the sixteenth centuries," the Common Service skipped over the Enlightenment and Pietism, and passed on a tradition that was almost contemporaneous with Luther.

Because it was adopted by almost all synods, from the Swedes and the Norwegians to the Germans, including the Missouri and Wisconsin synods, the Common Service was a near-miracle of Lutheran unity, something that has not yet had the scholarly attention it deserves.

That unity began to dissipate in 1958, the year the *Service Book and Hymnal* began to introduce ecumenical ceremonies. Historians will be able to trace how, alas, that unity was compromised, and how cooperation with the Missouri Synod was frittered away by those intent on being "ecumenical."

> **Because it was adopted by almost all synods ... the Common Service was a near-miracle of Lutheran unity, something that has not yet had the scholarly attention it deserves.**

For Discussion

1. Is an appeal to Luther's authority sectarian?

2. What practical effect did emphasis on the "simple sense" of Jesus' command have?

3. Does the Common Service represent the authentic tradition?

4. What is the alternative to "receptionism"?

5. What is the difference between "presiding over" and "administering" the sacrament?

Chapter 4

The Church's Supper

Supper of Christians

"The formal exegetical statement that the disciples are the subject of the imperative, 'This do,'" wrote Leonard Fendt, "does not justify making the Lord's Supper into the Supper of Christians."[91]

By "Supper of Christians" Fendt meant not acknowledging God's initiative in the Lord's Supper, but rather conducting the sacrament *as if it were something the church does.*

The Authority of the Eucharistic Prayer

Not long before the Council of Trent, Suffragan Bishop Michael Helding of Mainz claimed that the eucharistic prayer (the mass canon) had apostolic authority.

> I am certain of this, and can explain it with good grounds, that in the first apostolic church the true and holy body and the salutary blood of Christ in the eucharist had the name and also the action called "mass" and that both the name and the action have been maintained in the church everywhere up until our time.
>
> We know ... that the canon [eucharistic prayer] has been preserved from the time of the apostles absolutely word for word and that all the words of the canon ... are found in the books of those who lived and wrote a thousand years ago.[92]

91 *Einführung in die Liturgiewissenschaft* (Berlin: Alfred Töpelmann, 1958), 85.

92 *Von der Hailigsten Messe, Fünffzehn Predige zu Augspurg auff dem Richstag im Jar M.D.LLVIII. gepredigt, Durch Michaelen Bischoff zu Sidonien, Meinzischen Suffraganeen* (Ingolstadt 1548), Cr.

By "Supper of Christians" Fendt meant not acknowledging God's initiative in the Lord's Supper, but rather conducting the sacrament *as if it were something the church does.*

> **Synonyms:**
> Canon of the mass
> Mass canon
> Eucharistic prayer
> Great Thanksgiving
> The Prayer of Thanksgiving

Historians of the liturgy who have traced its gradual development, have long since rejected Helding's argument. The Council of Trent did not go so far as to claim apostolic authority for the prayer. Instead it mentioned apostolic *tradition*.

> ... the Catholic church instituted ... many centuries ago the holy canon, which is so free from error that it contains nothing that does not in the highest degree savor of a certain holiness and piety and raise up to God the minds of those who offer. For it consists partly of the very words of the Lord, partly of the traditions of the Apostles, and also of pious regulations of holy pontiffs.[93]

Here we find the origin of the "ecumenical consensus." The Council of Trent supported what we can call a "Supper of Christians," because it required that *the consecration of the bread and wine had to include human words*. Thus, erroneously, the Sacrament of the Altar is called a sacrifice—*something that the church does*.

Martin Chemnitz, one of the authors of the Formula of Concord, spotted the difference.

> ... the fourth Tridentine chapter [chapter from Council of Trent] does not dare simply to assert that the canon of the Mass was composed by Christ and the apostles, but says [merely] that the Catholic Church instituted it.[94]

Despite many attempts, there is no way to compromise between Roman Catholic and Lutheran teaching about direction.

- There is no possible compromise between down and up.
- There is no possible compromise between downward and upward.
- There is no possible compromise between the Lord's Supper and the Church's Supper. Listen to Luther:
  > ... so it is a contradiction in terms to call the mass a sacrifice, for the former is something we receive and the latter is something that we give. The same thing cannot be received and offered at the same time...[95]

---

[93] *The Canons and Decrees of the Sacred and Oecumenical Council of Trent*, H. J. Schroeder, ed. (St. Louis and London: Herder, 1950).

[94] Martin Chemnitz, *Examination of the Council of Trent, Part II* (St. Louis: Concordia, 1987), 509.

[95] LW 36:52.

Instead of accepting the "ecumenical consensus," Lutheran theologians should be at work convincing the rest of Christendom that the initiator of the sacrament is God himself, and that Jesus' sacred words of institution are not meant to be one paragraph in a longer prayer, reminding God of what he already knows. *There is no way to compromise between Roman Catholic and Lutheran teaching about direction.*

Embarassing Question

The Council of Trent also decreed that *the church's sacrifice is the same as the sacrifice on Calvary*, only in a different mode.

> For the victim is one and the same, *the same now offering by the ministry of priests who then offered himself on the cross*, the manner alone of offering being different.[96]

The members of the council went home, leaving the embarrassing question unanswered: *How can the mass be the same as the crucifixion?*

Participating in the Crucifixion

During the centuries following the Council of Trent in thousands of confirmation classes, Lutheran pastors have asked that question: *How can the mass be the same as the crucifixion?*

But the question is now out-of-date. There is a new answer, an astonishing new Roman Catholic teaching. Call it *ebenbildlich Gedenk-opfer* (commemorative sacrifice) or *Vergegenwärtigung* (contemporization, present re-actualization). The most common term is *Representatio*. One thing is clear: Lutheran pastors can no longer say that Catholic priests sacrifice Jesus Christ *again*.

The new idea is not that Jesus is sacrificed again, but rather that Jesus is always dying. Lutherans, of course, believe Hebrews 9.25-26, that Jesus died just *once*:

> Nor was it to offer himself repeatedly, as the high priest enters the Holy Place yearly with blood not his own, for then he would have had

[96] *The Canons and Decrees*, 146.

to suffer repeatedly since the foundation of the world. But as it is, he has appeared *once for all* at the end of the age to put away sin by the sacrifice of himself.

So how can the mass be the same as the crucifixion? After all, the crucifixion happened almost twenty centuries ago!

German monk Odo Casel, leader of a movement called "mystery theology," found the answer in Greek mystery cults. On a book flyleaf, Gerhardus van der Loewe called Casel "the most important theologian of the last hundred and fifty years, with the possible exception of Karl Barth."

For this new doctrine, common sense about death is not a hindrance. Time can be abolished. Discussing the "abolition of time through the imitation of archetypes," Mircea Eliade explains how the pagans did it.

> A sacrifice, for example, not only exactly reproduces the initial sacrifice revealed by a god *ab origine*, at the beginning of time, it also takes place at that same primordial mythical moment. In other words, every sacrifice repeats the initial sacrifice and coincides with it.[97]

Applied to the church, that means that during the mass, chronological time no longer exists. Believers are transported to Mount Calvary itself. Casel explained:

> In the mystery cult the epiphany goes on and on in worship; the saving, healing act of God is performed over and over. Worship is the means of making it real once more, and thus of breaking through to the spring of salvation. The members of the cult present again and again in ritual, symbolic fashion, that primeval act; in holy words and rites of priest and faithful the reality is there once more.... Thereby they win a share in the new life of God; they enter his chorus, they become gods. The mysteries' way, therefore, is the way of ritual action as sharing in the god's acts; its aim is union with the godhead, share in his life.[98]

It is absurd, of course, to argue that a "one-time sacrifice" can be "contemporized." But many clever theologians think it can. One dissertation called it the "way of ritual action as sharing in the god's acts," "a contemporization of the one-time sacrifice of Christ on the cross in the form of an image."[99] Translated into plain language, Christians can participate in the crucifixion, because *Jesus' death is still going on.* Since the death is still happening, the contemporary sacrifice of the mass, which includes the self-

---

[97] *Cosmos and History. The Myth of the Eternal Return* (New York: Harper and Row, 1959), 35.

[98] *The Mystery of Christian Worship and Other Writings* (Westminster, Md. Newman Press, 1962), 53.

[99] Erich Feifel, *Grundzüge einer Theologie des Gottesdienstes. Motive und Konzeption der Glaubensverkündigung Michael Heldings (1506–1561) als Ausdruck einer "Katholischen Reformation"* (Freiburg, et al.: Herder, 1960), 182.

sacrifice of the individual believer, can be combined with Jesus' sacrifice.

Mystery theologians were rebuked by Pope Pius XII (1876–1958):

> It is perfectly clear how much modern writers are wanting in the genuine and true liturgical spirit who, deceived by the illusion of a higher mysticism, dare to assert that attention should be paid not to the historic Christ, but to a "pneumatic" or glorified Christ.[100]

Pius XII to the contrary, however, according to the Vatican decree, *Sacrosanctum Concilium*, believers "take part in the sacrifice."[101]

According to prominent Roman Catholic theologian Karl Rahner:

> … the church has been entrusted by Christ with the power to celebrate liturgically Christ's sacrifice on the cross precisely in order that the Church may enter by faith and live into this action of its head … the visible sign of its simultaneous co-offering by the Body of Christ with its head.[102]

According to Roman Catholic theologian Charles Davis, the important matter is not justification by faith.

> But our union with Christ is not established simply by faith in his message, but by effectual contact with his redemptive acts. The saving activity by which the Church continues the work of Christ does not consist solely in the Word as preached, but in the Word as sacramentally efficacious. So, in our assembly, the reading and preaching of the Word is followed by the eucharistic celebration, in which the mystery of Christ's redemptive work is sacramentally renewed, *so that we can take part in it.*[103]

It is true that Christians are related to Jesus' death. According to Romans 6.3f.:

> Do you not know that all of us who have been baptized into Christ Jesus were baptized into his death? We were buried therefore with him by baptism into death, so that as Christ was raised from the dead by the glory of the Father, we too might walk in newness of life.

But Saint Paul clearly knew that Jesus died only once, not perpetually. Being "buried … into death," is quite different from "participating" in that death. In the Romans passage there is no hint of believers doing anything at all.

---

100 *Encyclical Letter of His Holiness Pius XII on the Sacred Liturgy (Mediator Dei)* (Washington: National Catholic Welfare Conference), n.d. 56.

101 *Sacrosanctum Concilium*, Pope Paul IV (Dec. 14, 1963), 1:10.

102 Karl Rahner and Angelus Haussling, *The Celebration of the Eucharist* (New York: Herder and Herder, 1968), 30.

103 *Liturgy and Doctrine: The Doctrinal Basis of the Liturgical Movement* (New York: Sheed and Ward, 1960), 69f [emphasis added].

Saint Paul clearly knew that Jesus died only once, not perpetually.

"Participating in the crucifixion," or "sharing in the redeeming deed," fits in with Roman Catholic doctrine of baptism, which is about ontological change, a new habitus (nature). Free from sin, a Christian is fit to be part of the Body of Christ, and thus take part in the crucifixion. Lutherans, on the contrary, believe that a Christian is "justified and a sinner at the same time" (*simul justus et peccator*). Clearly, a sinner cannot "participate" in the crucifixion!

Casel admits that "sharing in the redeeming deed" is different from Lutheran teaching.

> Christ's salvation must be made reality in us. *This does not come about through a "justification" from "faith" or by an application of the grace of Christ,* where we have only to clear things out of the way in a negative fashion to receive it. Rather, *what is necessary is a living, active sharing in the redeeming deed of Christ.*[104]

Our Sacrifice Must Be Separate from Christ's

Swedish theologian Bertil Garner made the Lutheran doctrine clear: Sinners cannot participate in Christ's sacrifice.

> Man's oblation, his offerings of thanks and praise, have always made a part of the celebration of the eucharist, but these spiritual sacrifices may not be mixed with the one sacrifice of Christ. We have to distinguish between these two kinds of sacrifice because one has to do with our offerings to God, the other with a receiving of the fruits of Christ's offering. In the New Testament eucharistic texts we never find a combination of Christ's sacrifice and ours, his unique offering once and for all and our self-oblation or spiritual sacrifice.[105]

Lutherans Convinced by Mystery Theology

Still, some Lutherans are convinced by the mystery theologians. In a preview of *Lutheran Book of Worship* (*LBW*), Eugene Brand asserted that the crucifixion was "present."

> **Lutherans ... believe that a Christian is "justified and a sinner at the same time" (*simul justus et peccator*). Clearly, a sinner cannot "participate" in the crucifixion!**

[104] *The Mystery of Christian Worship and Other Writings* (Westminster, Md.: Newman Press, 1962), 14, 52 [emphasis added].

[105] *Lutherans and Catholics in Dialog III* (USA Committee for Lutheran World Federation, 1967), 25.

Chapter 4 • The Church's Supper

> The primary note of the Service will be thanksgiving, that it will truly be a celebration of God's mighty work of redemption, a celebration not of past event, but of present reality.[106]

The logical meaning of "present reality," of course, is that Jesus never stops dying.

Even before the ELCA merger the ALC had swallowed the mysterious notion that Jesus' *action* is the church's *action*—and no one objected.

> It [the sacrament] is *anamnesis* [memory], a word rendered somewhat inadequately as "memorial." This means not only a reminder of Jesus' life and death, but the present re-actualization (becoming a present reality) of God's deed in Christ. It is the projection of God's saving act into the present life of the congregation.[107]

Schattauer's Conversion

Obviously, use of the eucharistic prayers in *Evangelical Lutheran Worship* will not alter piety overnight. The erosion, rather, will take place gradually, in the long-term, week after week, year after year, in books and articles, in relationships with other churches, and in explanations of the new "rite."

The change will be quicker in congregations that call pastors recently trained at Wartburg Seminary, since they learn there about "eucharistic piety" from liturgics professor, Thomas H. Schattauer. Schattauer does not (yet!) talk about "participating" in the crucifixion. But in unusually unguarded language he confessed how he abandoned Lutheran doctrine. He thereby delivered advance evidence about what the future effect of the *ELW* eucharistic prayers will be.

Attending 1977 lectures at Notre Dame University Schattauer heard German professor Wolfhart Pannenberg announce that "the rediscovery of the eucharist may prove to be the most important event in Christian spirituality of our time."[108]

"Eucharistic piety," Pannenberg said, is replacing "penitential piety," which was guilty of something that Pannenberg called "self-aggression." Schattauer saw the light. "Whereas my former liturgical piety was peniten-

In the New Testament eucharistic texts we never find a combination of Christ's sacrifice and ours …

---

106 "The Theological Basis for Liturgical Renewal," *The National Lutheran* (September, 1964): 13f.

107 "Statement on Communion Practices. A Statement Adopted by the Fourth General Convention of the American Lutheran Church" (October 1968), 2.

108 Thomas H. Schattauer, *Inside Out: Worship in an Age of Mission* (Minneapolis: Augsburg Fortress, 1999), 6ff.

tial, individual, retrospective and institutional ... the newly-emerging piety was eucharistic, communal, prospective and symbolic." His conversion, he reports, was "a reorientation of Christian piety away from a narrow focus on the individual entangled in sin and toward the church, from matters of personal salvation and devotion to matters of the liturgical assembly."

The Benefit of Eating and Drinking

To understand what is going on here, we have to realize that both Brand and Schattauer are attacking the Small Catechism.

> **Question:** What is the benefit of such eating and drinking?
> **Answer:** The words "given for you" and "shed for you" for the forgiveness of sins" show us that forgiveness of sin, life, and salvation are given to us in the sacrament through these words, because where there is forgiveness of sins, there is also life and salvation.

"Whereas the old piety had its origin in the medieval practice of penance," Schattauer continues, "this new piety had its source in a renewed practice of the eucharist." The eucharist has "communal, sacrificial, and eschatological dimensions." The "assembly" is the "symbolic enactment" of "God's eschatological purposes...."

"It would be difficult," he writes, "to identify the point where my own liturgical piety began to shift...." He made clear, however, that his abandonment of the catechism was influenced by the 1978 *Lutheran Book of Worship*. "I noted and welcomed the absence of the words, *by nature sinful and unclean*."

Chapter 4 • The Church's Supper

For Discussion

1. What is meant by "Supper of Christians"? How is it distinguished from the "Lord's Supper"?

2. How did Roman Catholics explain the mass following the Council of Trent? What is their new explanation? What is the Lutheran explanation?

3. What is "mystery theology"?

Chapter 5

Ecumenical Authority?

Liturgical changes will be the window through which the wolf will enter the evangelical fold—Matthias Flacius

The bright vision of a united Christendom has never completely faded. After Vatican Council II it shines again. The Roman Catholic Church is cautiously taking on features of the Reformation. Congregations are emphasizing Bible study, often putting some Lutheran congregations to shame. Most astonishing, the Latin mass is now said in English, and it is often difficult to tell the difference between Roman Catholic and Lutheran services. One aftereffect of the council was a lively movement called Liturgical Renewal. It impressed editor Eugene Brand of the *Lutheran Book of Worship*.

> It would hardly be an exaggeration to say that the common liturgy for a united Anglican, Lutheran, Roman Catholic church is already there.[109]

By 1958 Lutheran churches in the U.S.A. had reached a historical high-point of liturgical unity in the Common Service. But in that same year, the Lutheran *Service Book and Hymnal,* appeared, claiming "a clearer vision" and opening the door to "the rich treasure of ecumenical liturgy" (*SBH*, vii). Through that opened door the 1978 *Lutheran Book of Worship* moved "into the larger ecumenical heritage of liturgy" (*LBW*, 8), and away from Lutheran doctrine. According to its editor, the "historically-conditioned" Reformation orders were no longer the model.

By 1958 Lutheran churches in the U.S.A. had reached a historical high-point of liturgical unity in the Common Service.

109 Eugene L. Brand, "Die Erneuerung des Gottesdienstes. Zur liturgischen Arbeit in den lutherischen Kirchen," *Lutherische Monatshefte* (April 1987): 170.

The Lutheran heritage of worship, therefore, embraces and affirms the whole Christian tradition; its development should not be limited by non-critical adoption of such historically conditioned material as the church orders of the 16th century.[110]

Ecumenical commitment was mandated by the ecumenical nature of the liturgical tradition itself. From our beginnings, we Lutherans remained within the liturgical tradition, and no matter what the Lutheran confessions may imply, the liturgical tradition is a major component of the tradition of the church.[111]

In 2002, in *Principles for Worship* the editors for the developing ELCA hymnal appealed once more to a "growing ecumenical consensus."[112]

Roman Catholic scholar Charles Davis emphasizes that "liturgical renewal" bring doctrinal changes.

> We are dealing with a very extensive doctrinal revival ... We need, then, to set to work to spread abroad the doctrinal insights that motivate the desire for liturgical reform ... Serious reflection is required on our part to make our own the doctrinal progress that underlies the liturgical movement ... Let no one, then, underestimate the significance and power of the liturgical movement ... the concern is not with incidentals, but with the fundamentals of doctrine.[113]

What doctrines do they think need changing? In 2006 the hymnal *Evangelical Lutheran Worship* appeared—the third hymnal based on ecumenical authority. Because of that strange authority, we are now three steps away from where we were in 1958. Is the wolf entering the evangelical fold?

There have been warnings. "Clever opponents of Protestant teaching," Eduard Böhl wrote, "can only too easily make use of ceremonies to paralyze or destroy the church through the back door."[114] Agreement about ceremonies, Luther cautioned, is not possible without prior doctrinal agreement. God's grace, he insisted, must also govern the liturgy.

> For this is the true God who gives and does not receive, who helps and does not let himself be helped ... in short, he does and gives everything, and he has the need of no one; he does things freely out of pure grace without merit for the unworthy and undeserving, yes, for the damned and lost.[115]

Agreement about ceremonies, Luther cautioned, is not possible without prior doctrinal agreement.

---

110 Eugene L. Brand, ed., *Worship among Lutherans*, Northfield Statement on Worship, 1983; Tantur Report on Worship, 1981; (Geneva: Department of Studies, The Lutheran World Federation, 1983): 12 [emphasis added].

111 Eugene L. Brand, "Liturgical Reconnaissance," Nov. 18, 1998, http://www.wordalone.org/docs/wa-liturgical-reconnaissance.shtml [emphasis added].

112 *Renewing Worship, Vol. 2: Principles of Worship* (Augsburg Fortress: Minneapolis, 2002), iv [hereafter PW].

113 Charles Davis, *Liturgy and Doctrine: The Doctrinal Basis of the Liturgical Movement* (New York: Sheed and Ward, 1960), 200.

114 *Beiträge zur Geschichte der Reformation in Österreich* (Jena: Gustav Fischer, 1902), 16.

115 LW 38:107.

Chapter 5 • Ecumenical Authority?

Unneeded Rituals

Happily, some ceremonies discussed in the ELCA's *Principles for Worship* are not yet being urged on us. The new book does not yet call for "stational liturgies" or for the "veneration of the cross" (because of "the power of this saving sign") or for tabernacles (aumbries) used to store consecrated bread (*PW,* 84, 86, 85).

In spite of the Small Catechism's warning that water does not do such great things, the *ELW* shows an unhealthy interest in water.

> *It is not the water that does these things, but the word of God conneccted with the water and our faith which relies on that word of God. For without the word of God, it is simply water and not baptism.*
>
> LUTHER'S SMALL CATECHISM

Hymn 446 in the *ELW* reads, "my head is wet and I'm on my way." Recommending the *ELW*, Pastor Robert Rimbo of Trinity Church in Manhattan, predicts that "Your assembly will be very wet."[116] Hymn 455 includes "crashing water," "parting water," "cleansing water" and "living water." *Evangelical Lutheran Worship* lauds the waters of creation, the water on the mountains, springs in the valley, water in Noah's flood, water from the rock in the wilderness, water of the Jordan river, and rivers generally—of oceans, lakes, streams, cloud, rain, dew, snow, not forgetting Hagar's well and the water that washed Naaman (*ELW*, 70-71). But, as the Small Catechism cautions, "It is not the water" that does such great things, "but the word of God connected with the water, and our faith which relies on that word of God. For without the word of God, it is simply water and not baptism."

For the moment we are free from "touching the water in the font" (*PW,* 76), which apparently awaits a separate book of occasional services. "What difference might it make, if, on a daily basis," asks the *ELW* committee, "you prayed over water?"[117] The obvious answer to the absurd question: No difference at all.

"What difference might it make, if, on a daily basis," asks the *ELW* committee, "you prayed over water?" The obvious answer to the absurd question: No difference at all.

116 Robert Rimbo, "Worship Whys: Assembly Required," *The Lutheran,* September, 2006, 41.

117 *With the Whole Church: A Study Guide for Renewing Worship* (Minneapolis: Augsburg Fortress, 2005), 47.

Evangelical Lutheran Worship is also enamored with holy water. Repeatedly it introduces the *asperges* ritual: "As a reminder of the gift of baptism the assembly may be sprinkled with water during the singing" (*ELW*, 97, 119, 307, 308). A reminder perhaps, but since most Lutherans are baptized as infants, how many of them can remember their baptism?

But most often holy water has acted as a magnet for superstition: protection against sterility, the plague, and the devil and, at worst, promising remission of sins.[118]

At the time of the Reformation the formula was forbidden: *aqua benedicta deleat tua dilecta sit tibi*, "may the holy water blot out your sins, and be to you salvation and life."[119]

Until "liturgical renewal" came around, holy water has been banned in evangelical Lutheran churches, and we have no need for it today.

There is no apparent need for other ceremonies either, such as Affirmation of Christian Vocation, Welcome to Baptism, or "Thanksgiving for Baptism. Inventing unneeded ceremonies is not new. Martin Luther observed:

> Thus in the church of the New Testament heretics immediately followed the apostles. Likewise bishops who did not know the Lord. Later came the monks, and finally the entire papacy and the whole sacrilege stand in the holy place. And all these cried out: "Let us serve God somewhat more ardently and with greater piety! For the apostles overlooked much that must be added to the church; the fathers had too little in the way of devotion and ceremonies. *Let us accumulate more rites and acts of worship!*" In this manner ceremonies were increased in the church, for the devil mixed truth with falsehood, and the descendants gradually rushed into what was worse.[120]

Assault on Baptism

There is a tendency abroad, already evident in *LBW*, to make baptism, too, a liturgical action of the church, rather than God's action. There is nothing wrong with baptism at the Sunday service, but there is something wrong with the notion that it *must* be at Sunday service.[121]

There is a tendency abroad, already evident in *LBW*, to make baptism, too, a liturgical action of the church, rather than God's action.

---

118 Alfons Kirchgässner, *Die Mächtigen Zeichen. Ursprünge, Formen und Gesetze des Kultes. Basel* (Frieburg, Wien: Herder, 1959), 530

119 *Verlegung der Apologia Sydoni damit er seinen Catechismum verteidiget* (Magdeburg: Christian Rödiger, 1553), B v\.

120 WA 44:676 [emphasis added].

121 Jeffrey A. Truscott, *The Reform of Baptism and Confirmation in American Lutheranism*, Drew University Studies in Liturgy II (Lanham, Maryland & Oxford: Scarecrow Press, 2003), 33, 205.

Chapter 5 • Ecumenical Authority?

"Baptism," according to *Evangelical Lutheran Worship*, "is set within the principal gathering for worship" (*ELW*, 7). That rubric could signal the beginning of a new doctrine that the *assembly* plays a necessary role in validating baptism (*ELW*, 237).

Baptism, however, does not require assent by the assembly. The actor in baptism is God alone, and so it can be administered at any time, inside or outside of the assembly.

Since the New Testament recognizes neither holy places nor the pagan notion of "auspicious" times, Lutherans must be suspicious of the Easter Vigil (*ELW*, 266), billed as "an especially ancient and appropriate time for baptism" (*PW*, 99, 114, 121). There is no "especially appropriate time" for baptism.

Assault on Confirmation

There is a new saying out there: "Confirmation is a rite in search of a theology."[122] It comes from embarrassed Roman Catholic historians, who realize that the "Sacrament of Confirmation" is a ceremony originally part of baptism. The reaction of the Lutheran church should be "we told you so!"

[122] Anita Staufer, "Baptism: Back to the Future," *Currents in Theology and Mission* 30 (2003): 376.

> Lutherans long ago *abolished* the "Sacrament of Confirmation."
>   It did not meet Saint Augustine's criteria for a sacrament:
>   (1) Jesus' command, and
>   (2) a physical element: wine, bread, or water.
> The Lutheran church developed a wholly separate and unrelated *system of instruction* for children, also (unfortunately) called confirmation.

The same name for two very different things is unfortunate. In German there is a difference between Roman Catholic *Firmung* and Lutheran *Konfirmation*. Lutheran confirmation is not a *rite*, but a system for instructing children, long since deeply imbedded in folk custom. Voices were heard long ago recommending that catechization be practiced not just once, but repeatedly.

Voices were heard long ago recommending that catechization be practiced not just once, but repeatedly.

The system is very successful. The East German communists even felt it necessary to compete with confirmation by means of their *Jugendweihe*, or "youth consecration." And at the age of 13, children from the Australian Outback, for instance, regularly (and sometimes at great expense) report for instruction to Lutheran pastors.

- The ceremony called "Affirmation of Baptism" (*ELW*, 234) is meant to replace confirmation. [123]

Furthermore, even the practice of First Communion is in dangerous territory. The *LBW: Minister's Desk Edition* attacks public catechesis related to confirmation. Coming to communion for the first time, it says, "should not be blurred by loading it down with such embellishments as public catechesis, vows, white robes, or group song." But catechesis is not an *embellishment*. It is an integral part of instruction of children.

Our church should not be led to abandon our venerable confirmation practice by imitating the Roman Catholic program of downplaying the "Sacrament of Confirmation," or because of the (mistaken) notion that public catechesis is an "embellishment."[124]

No Biblical Mandate

There is no biblical mandate for "sprinkling with water" or for the "lighting of a new fire" (*ELW*, 266). And there is just as little mandate for foot washing (*ELW*, 260) as there is for a ceremony of cursing fig trees. About ceremonies, Apology XXIV 92 stipulates, "Without the authority of Scripture it is not safe to institute forms of worship in the church."

Nor is there any mandate from Jesus for unction or chrism, that is, application of oil (*ELW*, 231, 273, 276, 277). James 5.14 reads: "Is any one among you sick? Let them call for the elders of the church, and let them pray over him, anointing him with oil in the name of the Lord." Here, James is only giving medical advice. We should send up a cheer that Roman Catholics agree: *unction* is no longer called *extreme*. Neither James' advice nor the mention of oil in Mark 6.13 is a divine mandate to the church. They are merely

---

[123] Jeffrey Truscott, "The Reform of Baptism and Confirmation in American Lutheranism" [Drew University Studies in Liturgy No. 11] (Lanham, Maryland & Oxford: The Scarecrow Press, 2003), 127-204.

[124] *Lutheran Book of Worship: Minister's Desk Edition* (Minneapolis: Augsburg Publishing House, 1978), 31-32.

Without the authority of Scripture it is not safe to institute forms of worship in the church.

Chapter 5 • Ecumenical Authority?

descriptions of "apostolic usage," certainly not a means by which God forgives sins. "Apostolic usage," in fact, is no longer possible after the deaths of the apostles.

It is impossible to do it now according to apostolic usage; the dear apostles healed the sick with their shadows (Acts 5), with oil (Mark 6, 13; James 5), with their handkerchiefs and aprons (Acts 19), and by other means.[125]

125 Matthias Flacius, *Widder den auszug des Leipsischen Interims, oder das kleine Interim* (Magdeburg: Christian Rödinger, 1549), [Aiiij r].

The Calendar

The lengthy *ELW* calendar is also less than evangelical and requires separate treatment. To give only a couple examples, it is bad judgment to recognize the feast of Julian of Norwich (*ELW*, 15), whose writing is more Neo-platonist than Christian, or to sing Julian's feminist hymn, "Mothering God, You Gave Me Birth" (*ELW*, hymn 735). Holy Cross Day, September 14 (*ELW*, 16) is a foolish commemoration since there is small chance that the relic exhibited in 629 A.D. by the Emperor Heraclius after recovering it from the Persians (the origin of the feast) was really the "true cross."

> **Examining *ELW* hymns, one notices that masculine words have vanished during the "careful crafting of texts to minimize the use of gender-specific pronouns for God."**

Tampering with the Bible Text

More unacceptable still, *Evangelical Lutheran Worship* has tampered with the Bible text itself. Examining *ELW* hymns, one notices that masculine words have vanished during the "careful crafting of texts to minimize the use of gender-specific pronouns for God" (*PW*, 13). Its pronoun police have reduced 451 occurrences in the psalms of the masculine pronoun *he* to 19, and 468 occurrences of *his* to 50.

> **Psalm 23**—*He restores my soul; he leads me in paths of righteousness.*
> **ELW**—*You restore my soul, O Lord, and guide me along right pathways.*

Their plea that they are providing "a version intended for common sung prayer and proclamation, rather than a translation for study" (*ELW*, 335) will not do. There is nothing unsingable about the pronoun *he*. Obviously the editors were not concerned primarily with enhancing "sung prayer" and "proclamation," but with placating feminists. Theirs is not a translation, but a paraphrase.

Evangelical Lutheran Worship also dares to tamper with the creeds, a grave offence, as church history witnesses. The ancient words, "He was made man," in the Nicene Creed, appear as "became truly human." A footnote explains the words "and from the Son" (*filioque*) are a "later addition" without mentioning that the Lutheran church is committed to that addition. In the Apostles' Creed, "his only Son, our Lord," becomes "God's only Son, our Lord." "Descended into hell," becomes "descended to the dead."[126]

Use of the Apocrypha

The *ELW* also errs by authorizing selections from the Apocrypha. "We teach and confess," reads the Formula of Concord, "that the only rule and guiding principle according to which all teachings and teachers are to be evaluated and judged are the prophetic and apostolic writings of the Old and New Testaments alone...."

The Apocrypha belongs neither to the Old or the New Testaments, but to another category that the Formula calls "other writings of ancient or contemporary teachers, whatever their names may be." They "shall not be regarded as equal to Holy Scriptures, but all of them together shall be subjected to it...."[127]

In spite of the confessional warning, *ELW* dares to prescribe "other writings," Baruch (*ELW*, 19), The Wisdom of Jesus Son of Sirach (*ELW*, 21, 24, 25, 38, 46, 51), and The Wisdom of Solomon (*ELW*, 21, 42, 48, 52, 59, 61).

But whether read or sung, the church of the Word cannot tolerate unreliable words—either from the *ELW*'s psalter, however "carefully crafted," or from the unreliable Apocrypha.

---

126 Cf. Gotthold Doehler, "The Decent Into Hell," Springfielder 39 1-19, Concordia Journal 2 (1976): 43-47.

127 Formula of Concord, Epitome, Introduction [BC, 486].

Chapter 5 • Ecumenical Authority?

Doubtful Doctrine

The new *ELW* hymnal authorizes prayers for the dead:

> Into your hands, O merciful Savior, we commend your servant, (name). Acknowledge, we humbly beseech you, a sheep of your own fold, a lamb of your own flock, a sinner of your own redeeming. *Receive her/him into the arms of your mercy*, into the blessed rest of everlasting peace, and into the glorious company of the saints in light (*ELW*, 283f, emphasis added).

Interestingly, *LBW* has an identical prayer on page 211. Prayer for the dead is not only useless; it offers false comfort by implying a second chance of salvation after death.

The prayer for "those whose marriage has ended" (*ELW*, 82) is inappropriate, since it appears to sanction divorce.

No Independent Review

In the introduction to *Evangelical Lutheran Worship* we read the cryptic statement that "In 2005 both church bodies [the ELCA and the ELCIC] affirmed the completion of Evangelical Lutheran Worship and commended its use" (*ELW*, 8).

But, in truth, at the 2005 ELCA assembly at Orlando, Florida, voting members had insufficient data to make informed decisions about the new hymnal. They approved only a "process," voting "that the Office of the Presiding Bishop through worship staff … complete the liturgical review of proposed content of a new book of worship."[128] No one saw the actual book.

In the past, Lutheran churches have been very cautious indeed about doctrine, every sentence, every word. In retrospect it is clear that the delegates at Orlando opened the door for breath-taking changes in doctrine that would have horrified our predecessors—altered creeds, a rewritten psalter, non-canonical readings, prayers for the dead, holy water, and most foreboding, departure from the Reformation through a changed

---

128 "2005 Churchwide Assembly: Reports and Records: Assembly Minutes," Evangelical Lutheran Church in America (Chicago: Office of the Secretary, ELCA, 2006), 144.

In retrospect it is clear that the delegates at Orlando opened the door for breathtaking changes in doctrine that would have horrified our predecessors—altered creeds, a rewritten psalter, non-canonical readings, prayers for the dead, holy water, and most foreboding, departure from the Reformation through a changed liturgical direction.

liturgical direction. Since Orlando the "process" has continued, and sales representatives have been instructed *not to discuss doctrine.*

The parliamentary procedure was technically correct, but unwise. Ironically, an assembly structured (against Article XIV of the Augsburg Confession) to be radically democratic surrendered wholesale doctrinal authority to a very small group. Constant use will trouble many faithful members as they gradually discover its many departures from Lutheran doctrine and practice.

It would have been better if the new hymnal had been submitted at least to some *independent judgment* as the *LBW* was compelled to do, following criticism from the ALC.[129]

Many voices recommend unity within the ELCA, but more important than unity is truth. It is time to listen to the warning of Matthias Flacius four-and-a-half centuries ago, "Liturgical changes will be the window through which the wolf will enter the evangelical fold."[130]

Nevertheless, our confessions remain superior to decisions of an assembly and each local church is responsible for choosing. After a half century of being influenced by "ecumenical consensus" it is time for local congregations to heed the ancient warning about the liturgy, "the law of praying is the law of believing": *lex orandi, lex credendi.*

---

[129] Ralph Quere, *In the Context of Unity: A History of the Development of the LBW* (Minneapolis: Lutheran University Press, 2003), 111-156.

[130] *Bulla Antichristi de retrahendohendo populo Dei in ferream Aegipiticae servitutis fornacem* (Magdeburg: Michael Lotter, 1549), A iij r.

Chapter 5 • Ecumenical Authority?

For Discussion

1. With regard to worship, what are the positive and the negative aspects of ecumenism?

2. How has the Roman Catholic understanding of the "Sacrament of Confirmation" affected our practice?

3. Since it is comforting for the mourners at a funeral, why not pray for the dead?

4. Since Lutherans have always been urged to read the Apocrypha, why should it not be read at Sunday service?
   Examine the books of Baruch, Sirach, and the Wisdom of Solomon.

5. What would make a hymnal "official"?

Chapter 6

The Eucharistic Prayer

The average churchgoer will hardly notice it, but those who have been alerted to the issues will understand that the worst doctrinal menace in the new *Evangelical Lutheran Worship* is the use of the "eucharistic prayer," which encircles Jesus' words of institution *so they are part of a prayer to God, and no longer Jesus' words to us.*

> **For examples of the eucharistic prayer see:**
> *Evangelical Lutheran Worship*
> - Versions I, III, IV (*ELW*, 108, 110, 111)
> - Versions V through XI (*ELW*, 65-70), where they are labeled "Thanksgiving at the Table"
>
> *Lutheran Book of Worship*
> - Rubric 31 (*LBW*, 69, 89, 110)
>
> *Service Book and Hymnal*
> - "The Prayer of Thanksgiving" (*SBH*, 34, 62)

The danger of the eucharistic prayer is not primarily its text, but its direction. The reversal of direction may not offend even pastors, since they are trained to be careful about textual statements, not about ceremonies.

The danger of the eucharistic prayer is not primarily its text, but its direction.

> **Synonyms:**
> Canon of the mass
> Mass canon
> Eucharistic prayer
> Great Thanksgiving
> The Prayer of Thanksgiving

Most important of all, our "giving eucharist" takes the place of God's forgiving. In turn, that change requires a different understanding of baptism. According to "eucharistic theology" baptism grants a new habitus or nature. Now the worshiper is no longer a sinner but innocent. (Hence, the Roman Catholic distinction between "mortal sins" and "venial sins.")

That understanding is contrary to the Lutheran formula, *simul justus et peccator*, "at the same time just and a sinner." Then, as a member of the Body of Christ, he goes to communion sinlessly to offer "eucharist." At the eucharistic prayer his self-sacrifice is merged with Christ's sacrifice. Thus at mass the believer participates in the crucifixion (as discussed in chapter 4).

No less than the "historic episcopate," the eucharistic prayer was a central goal of the Episcopalians when they began talks with the ELCA. In the 1982 Lutheran–Episcopal Agreement the ELCA accepted a requirement that in combined communion services only a eucharistic prayer would be permitted.

For profound reasons, Luther emphatically rejected that prayer. After his death, at a 1558 conference in Altzelle, Saxon theologians decided that it would be the most important matter of an ecumenical council.[129]

For centuries the "eucharistic prayer" (canon of the mass) has not been read in Lutheran churches.

For centuries the "eucharistic prayer" (canon of the mass) has not been read in Lutheran churches. It is essential that members of congregations make the effort to understand what is involved. "Here is clearly an area," according to William Rusch, "where the relation of theology to the liturgy is involved. There is not one mind in the church on these matters."[130]

Downward or Upward

Including human words in the consecration means enclosing the words of institution (like a sandwich) within a human prayer. Making the words of institution into part of a prayer results in a change of direction. That means that the liturgy is initiated by humans and directed to God.

---

129 *Corpus Reformatorum* (Berlin et al., 1834), 7:214 [hereafter CR].

130 William G. Rusch, "A Background Paper for a Theological Review of Materials" (Produced by the Inter-Lutheran Commission on Worship, Mimiographed, January, 1977): 31.

Chapter 6 • The Eucharistic Prayer

Keep in mind that Martin Luther taught that the Sacrament of the Altar is something that God does.

> Therefore these two things—mass and prayer, sacrament and work, testament and sacrifice—must not be confused; for the one comes from God to us through the ministration of the priest and demands our faith, the other proceeds from our faith to God through the priest and demands his hearing. The former descends, the later ascends.[131]

We Have Been Through This Before

It is not the first time the Lutheran church has been under hard ecumenical-liturgical pressure. The first time it was exerted by Holy Roman Emperor Charles V himself. After the Lutheran princes had been defeated on the battlefield only three years after Luther's death, the Interim Law of 1548 (Augsburg Interim) dictated restoration of Roman ceremonies. "They pressed hard," according to Philipp Melanchthon, "about the canon [eucharistic prayer]."[132] But the winning resistance recognized that liturgical uniformity was "enough in itself to bring back the papacy."[133] Now, oddly enough, in a democratic age we are being maneuvered to accept the same ceremonies Emperor Charles V could not force on the Lutheran church.

The Whole Papacy Is in the Canon

Far from being a liberal cause, the eucharistic prayer is very conservative, the very kernel of the power of clergy. The supposed power of priests to "consecrate" (*confect*) the sacrament not only has doctrinal consequences, but also powerful political consequences. Consider the following:

- "Human words" are essential in the eucharistic prayer.
- The prayer causes Christ's presence.
- Only the priest has the power to pray the eucharistic prayer.
- The priests authorized to pray that prayer possess special power.
- Those who possess the power to pray it therefore constitute a powerful priestly caste....

---

131 E. Theodore Bachman and Helmut T. Lehman, eds., *Luther's Works*, vol. 36 (Philadelphia: Muhlenberg Press, 1960), 56 [hereafter cited as *LW*].

132 Matthias Flacius, *Gründliche Verlegung aller Sophisterey, so D. Pfeffinger mit den andern Adiaphoristen das Leipzigsche Interim zubesdchönen, gebraucht* (Magdeburg: Christian Rödinger, 1551), C ij r. [Note: No careful student can deny the contemporary controversy about the canon is a continuation of the sixteenth-century controversy.]

The supposed power of priests to "consecrate" (*confect*) the sacrament not only has doctrinal consequences, but also powerful political consequences.

133 *Ein Brief der Prediger zu Hamburg an die Theologen zu Wittenbergk in welchem gehandelt wird von Mitteldingen zu dieser Zeit sehr nützlich zu lesen* (Magdeburg: Christian Rödinger, 1549), A iiij, C iij r.

It is not difficult to complete the thought. Reporting on one archbishop, the *New York Times* reported:

> Waxing eloquent on the unique power of priests to accomplish things that not even kings and queens could do, he reminded us that even God obeys the words of a priest when he consecrates the bread and wine at mass.[134]

It is not difficult to understand why the Church of Rome will never admit that Luther was right. Since that is the case, in the cause of unity some Lutherans have accepted the prayer, and have found many justifications.

The Fog of Adiaphora

Lutherans are liturgically vulnerable partly because of the Greek word *adiaphora* (indifferent matters). The word has made a permanent impression on theology students and pastors, causing them to think of liturgical matters as irrelevant, reserved for enthusiasts. In a kind of fog, Lutherans do not remember that ceremonies bring doctrines with them. For centuries everything liturgical tended to be considered *adiaphoron*, an indifferent matter. The typical question, instead, was whether one liked or disliked liturgy. "What kind of word is *adiaphora*?" someone wrote at the time of the Reformation. "I think the accursed devil himself invented it. Now everything is adiaphora, whether one prays to God or the devil."[135]

It is time to get things clear. Adiaphora have to do with the church's freedom.

True Freedom. When opponents have insisted on adiaphora as necessary, evangelical Lutherans have deliberately refused to agree, in the name of evangelical freedom.

- They said we had to break the bread, so evangelical–Lutherans (even the celebrant) use small breads that require no breaking.[136]
- They said we had to use fermented bread, so evangelical Lutherans use unfermented bread. Similarity to the unfermented bread of the Passover is mere coincidence. (The combination of fermented bread with intinction produces a disgusting mess that resembles the Last Supper not at all.)

---

134 Paul E. Dinter, "A Catholic Crisis: Bestowed from Above," *New York Times*, January 1, 2003.

135 *Ein Vermanung zur Bestendigkeit in bekentnis der warheit, Creutz und Gebett, in dieser betrübten zeit, sehr nützlich und tröstlich* (Magdeburg: Michael Loter, 1549), A iiij v.

136 The answer to the question of the Faith and Order Commission of the World Council of Churches, whether "the breaking of bread" is constitutive of the Sacrament of Holy Communion, *Baptism, Eucharist and Ministry* [Faith and Order Paper No. 111] (Geneva, 1982), 16.

> **In kind of a fog, Lutherans do not remember that ceremonies bring doctrines with them.**

If "wafers" do not seem much like bread, they can be baked with more heft, but there is no need to duplicate exactly the bread Jesus used.
- They say pastors have to be ordained by a bishop, so evangelical Lutherans recognize also presbyteral ordinations [ordination by pastors].

False Freedom. Many think that anything liturgical is an *adiaphon*, so anything goes. Theirs is a false freedom. But *adiaphora* was only one of the crucial words in the sixteenth-century controversy. There were two other important terms.
- *Mandata* (what is commanded). Our Nihil Rule explains what Jesus mandated, for example, "Take and eat."
- *Damnabilia* (what has to be condemned). Certain ceremonies cannot be accepted, for example, the Corpus Christi procession.

Change of Terminology

Some Lutherans have been convinced to accept the human words after a mere change of terminology. Pastors who would react negatively to talk about the "sacrifice of the mass," soon became accustomed to using the word *eucharist* (thanksgiving), the preferred term after Vatican II. Hardly anyone objected to the title, the "Great Thanksgiving" (*LBW*, 68). Before that, it was slipped into the *Service Book and Hymnal* as "The Prayer of Thanksgiving," (*SBH*, 34, 62).

"Scholarship"

According to the *Service Book and Hymnal*:
> … [as] our Churches in America have come more fully to appreciate each other, they have also discovered through deepened scholarship and broader fellowship the rich treasury of ecumenical liturgy.…[137]

It is naïve not to notice that the "deepened scholarship" and appreciation of the "rich ecumenical treasury of ecumenical liturgy" can be traced in large part to writers bound to the decrees of the Council of Trent. Protestant writers in England and Sweden, of course, also exerted some

---

137 *Service Book and Hymnal* (Minneapolis: Augsburg Pblishing House, 1958), vii.

> **Pastors who would react negatively to talk about the "sacrifice of the mass," soon became accustomed to using the word *eucharist* (thanksgiving), the preferred term after Vatican II.**

influence. "In reaching the decision to include a eucharistic prayer," according to William Rusch, "the commission for *SBH* was influenced by recent work in liturgical studies by such scholars as Brilioth, Dix, and Frere."[138]

Yngve Brilioth

The "ecumenical consensus," it appears, is not quite overwhelming. Among its Lutheran proponents, Brian Spinks of Churchill College, Cambridge, observed that "a careful examination of the footnotes and bibliographies of these works reveals an interesting fact. All make use of, or cite as authoritative, *a single work* by the Swedish Lutheran scholar, Bishop Yngve Brilioth."[139]

Peter Brunner

Peter Brunner, doctoral advisor at Heidelberg to Robert Jenson and Eugene Brand, echoing Odo Casel, wrote mysteriously:

> In the victorious power of Jesus' sacrificial death on the cross the New Testament covenant memorial ... ascends to God's throne and evokes his active, end-effecting remembering. Holy Communion, too, is not a passive, static "mystery" given us for "contemplation," but is a dynamic event. In its earthly administration it releases a heavenly event, a kingdom-of-God movement in the heavens, yes, even in the heart of God.[140]

In plain language Brunner is saying that a unique event can be "present." He has accepted Casel's argument that the crucifixion never ends, and that Jesus is always dying.

> In the worship of the church, the salvation-event, which took place once for all in the body of Jesus on Golgotha and is now eternally valid before God's throne, is really present.[141]

Brunner's illogical statement is embarrassing (and Concordia Publishing House should be embarrassed for printing it). Ernst Bizer called it "a completely new doctrine."[142]

Commanded by Jesus?

Robert Rimbo argues that "the eucharistic prayer, then, is the fulfillment of one part of Jesus' command...."[143]

---

[138] "A Background Paper for a Theological Review of Materials Produced by the Inter-Lutheran Commission on Worship," January 1977, Unpublished, 29.

[139] *Luther's Liturgical Criteria and his Reform of the Canon of the Mass* (Bramcote Notts: Grove Books, 1982), II. Italics added. Cf.; Yngve Brilioth, *Eucharistic Faith and Practice: Evangelical and Catholic* (London: SPCK, 1956).

[140] *Worship in the Name of Jesus,* (St. Louis: Concordia Publishing House, 2004), 192.

[141] Ibid. 645, note 227.

[142] "Lutherische Abendmahlslehre?" *Evangelische Theologie* 16 (1956): 10.

[143] Robert Rimbo, "Worship Whys: Thanksgiving," *The Lutheran,* November 2006, 41.

Chapter 6 • The Eucharistic Prayer

Gordon Lathrop, a proponent of a full eucharistic prayer in the Lutheran churches, argues that in the command "Do this," Jesus mandated prayer. But as we have seen, the Nihil Rule explains that Jesus' command, "Do this," means consecrating, distributing, receiving, eating, and drinking. *But not prayer.*

Remembrance (Greek, *anamnesis*) is eating and drinking, not prayer. "Nowhere," writes Timothy C. J. Quill, "is our giving of thanks mentioned as primary or essential to the Lord's Supper."[144] Jesus has nothing against prayer, but Rimbo and Lathrop are mistaken. *Jesus' command, "Do this," does not mandate prayer*—certainly not a "eucharistic" prayer.

Continuity with Pagan Worship

Evangelical theologians properly emphasize that Christ's institution is something new. Others disagree. The interpretation of the "eucharistic prayer" by *mystery* theology, as was discussed above, follows Casel, who calls Christian worship" a "fulfillment of the mystery ritual type."[145]

Continuity with the Seder

On the basis of the Hebrew prayers called *berakoth* and *hodayoth*, Gordon Lathrop contends that there is continuity between Christian worship and the Jewish seder (Passover meal). In a variation of the appeal to "ecumenical consensus," he invokes unspecified scholarship. "If on the basis of modern biblical studies," he writes, "we may now understood [sic] 'do this' and 'bless' or 'give thanks' more clearly than we have, we need not then be afraid to draw the ritual conclusions these studies imply."[146]

Hoping to promote understanding of Jewish neighbors, many churches have drawn those "ritual conclusions" and on Maundy Thursday celebrate a Seder meal [the Passover ceremony]. But there is something wrong with attempting to recover a ceremony of the Old Testament. Jesus drew a line

---

144 *The Impact of the Liturgical Movement on American Lutheranism* (Lanham, Md. & London: The Scarecrow Press, 1977), 55f.

145 *The Mystery of Christian Worship and Other Writings*, (Westminster, Md.: Newman press, 1962), 35, 52.

146 Gordon Lathrop, "The Prayers of Jesus and the Great Prayer of the Church," *Lutheran Quarterly* 26 (1974): 172.

> **Remembrance (Greek, *anamnesis*) is eating and drinking, not prayer.**

> **Jesus drew a line when he announced that his meal was new, that it offered "the New Testament in my blood" ... *there is no continuity between the Seder and the Last Supper.***

when he announced that his meal was new, that it offered "the new testament in my blood." Furthermore, Professor Mark Throntveit of Luther Seminary has demonstrated that *there is no continuity between the Seder and the Last Supper.*[147]

Continuity with the Early Church

Our theologians have shown nowhere near the enthusiasm for liturgical studies as others have. A result is the widespread assumption that Roman liturgy sets the standard. The 1958 *SBH* left the impression (1) that Luther's reform was slipshod and (2) that the eucharistic prayer is the standard.

> A vision clearer than was sometimes possible in the turmoil of the Reformation controversy has revealed the enduring value of some elements which were lost temporarily in the sixteenth century reconstruction of the liturgy, as, for instance, the proper use of the Prayer of Thanksgiving … [148]

The same assumption underlies an article by the editor of the 1978 *LBW* that in reforming the eucharistic prayer, Luther practiced illegitimate "surgery."[149] Now, the *ELW* committee tells us:

The present situation calls for a renewal of worship and of common resources for worship, a renewal grounded in the treasures of the church's history while open to the possibilities of the future.[150]

The truth is that the liturgical "treasures of the church's history" begin with the books written during the "Triumph of the Church" in the fourth century, the time of Emperor Constantine. Before that almost nothing survived. During the persecutions, the Roman police burned the church's books. So reconstructing the earlier tradition by patching together a few snippets from the Didache, the First Letter of Clement, Ignatius of Antioch, and Justin, simply cannot be done.

> The documents of the apostolic period brought together in the New Testament give us no exhaustive picture of the liturgy of their time. Even when one takes into consideration that at that time there could not have been agendas, because the liturgical action was not yet uniformly fixed, the New Testament is silent about much about which we

---

[147] 'The Lord's Supper as New Testament, Not New Passover." *Lutheran Quarterly* XI (1997): 271-289.

[148] SBH, vii.

[149] Eugene Brand, "Luther's Liturgical Surgery," *Interpreting Luther's Legacy,* Meuser & Schneider, eds. (Minneapolis: Augsburg, 1969), 108-119.

[150] PW, iv.

Our theologians have shown nowhere near the enthusiasm for liturgical studies as others have. A result is the widespread assumption that Roman liturgy sets the standard.

would like to know. *A clear picture is first afforded us by the fourth century, from which the oldest liturgical formulae have been transmitted to us.*[151]

Continuity with Early Lutheran Orders

The eucharistic prayer was favored by the King John III of Sweden (1573–1592) in his Red Book (1576), as Chicago pastor Frank Senn proved in his dissertation "Liturgia Svecanae Ecclesiae: An Attempt at Eucharistic Restoration during the Swedish Reformation."[152]

"Eucharistic Restoration" was also practiced by the Elector of Brandenburg[153] and by King Edward VI of England, whose "Lutheran" Prayer Book is listed by Arthur Carl Piepkorn, with ten other precedents.[154] Liturgical questions, however, must be decided on theological grounds, not on the basis of historical precedent.

Liturgical questions ... must be decided on theological grounds, not on the basis of historical precedent.

The Community of Taizé

Influential in many countries, and in America in many Lutheran university chaplaincies and especially at the Philadelphia Seminary, is the liturgy of the monastic community of Taizé in France, where the eucharistic prayer is always used. The argument that since it is used in an "ecumenical" community it is suitable for Protestants, however, is less convincing when one realizes that its founder and abbot, Roger Schutz, was a Roman Catholic. "Years ago the former Reformed pastor had converted to the Catholic faith, but following the wish of the deceased pope—apparently on ecumenical grounds—he never admitted it publicly. In the past, the 89-year-old Swiss had repeatedly taken communion in papal masses."[155]

Discovery of Liturgical Structure

According to the publication *Principles for Worship*, new information is available, including rules for proper liturgical construction.

> The past three decades have seen not only a growing ecumenical consensus but also a deepened focus on the church's mission to the world.

---

151 Rudolf Stählin, "Die Geschichte des christlichen Gottesdienstes von der Urkirche bis zur Gegenwargt," *Leiturgia: Handbuch des Evangelischen Gottesdienstes* I (Kassel: Johannes Stauda-Verlag, 1954), 6 [italics added].

152 Frank Senn, "Liturgia Svecanae Ecclesiae: An Attempt at Eucharistic Restoration during the Swedish Reformation," Doctoral dissertation, University of Notre Dame, 1979.

153 Nikolaus Müller, "Zur Geschichte des Interims," *Jahrbuch für Brandenburgische Kirchengeschichte*, 5 (1908): 51, 54.

154 "The New Liturgy (cont.)," *American Lutheran* 32 (1949): 8.

155 http://www.kreuz.net/article.981.html of 4/13/ 2005.

156 PW, iv.

The church has embraced broadened understanding of culture, increasing musical diversity, changes in the usage of language, a renewed understanding of the central pattern of Christian worship, and an explosion of electronic media and technologies.... [156]

The compilers of the *ELW* have not explained why that "renewed understanding" should take the place of the Nihil Rule. That Nihil Rule, to use their language, is "the central pattern of Christian worship" required of churches that have adopted the confessions.

Anamnesis and Epiclesis

To make sure we are all talking about the same thing, Christians, who speak most of the world's languages, insist on retaining a few standard Greek words. The backward-looking "central pattern" requires two elements within the eucharistic prayer, in Greek called *anamnesis* (remembrance) and *epiclesis* (invocation). Many liturgiologists rejoice that West and East have thus been united because the crucial "actions" respectively of the Western and Eastern church, have been brought together. Members of the Eastern Orthodox churches are told that the action of epiclesis is a "resurrection" of the (dead!) elements of bread and wine. Willing to adopt the ecumenical consensus, the *ELW* (without explaining why) prescribes *epiclesis*.

> ... with your Word and Holy Spirit to bless us, your servants, and these your own gifts of bread and wine (*ELW,* 109).

> Holy God, we long for your Spirit. Come among us. Bless this meal. (*ELW,* 110, 132)

> ... with your Word and Holy Spirit to bless us, your servants, with your own gifts of bread and wine (*ELW* p. 131).

> Pour out your Holy Spirit on us and on these gifts of bread and wine (*ELW,* 111, 133).

Those who, like Luther, reject the notion that worship is human "action," do not agree. These invocations of the Holy Spirit are contrary to Lutheran theology. The sacrament is valid, not because the Holy Spirit descends, but because Christ's death activates his testament. The Western church emphasizes remembering (Greek, *anamnesis*) his death. Remembering is done by eating and drinking. "Thy testamental cup I take," reads hymn 266 (*SBH*), "and thus remember thee."

"Christ speaks," according to Luther, that "we should eat his body and drink and thus remember him. ..."[157]

But eating and drinking do not seem to be exactly what *ELW* has in mind, when they use words taken from the Latin mass canon. How otherwise than drinking, can we use a "cup" to remember?

> With this bread and cup we remember our Lord's Passover (*ELW*, 111).
> With this bread and cup we remember your Word dwelling among us (*ELW*, 110, 132).

Mention in the Apology

It has been argued that because the word *eucharist* appears in Apology of the Augsburg Confession XXIV:76 that Melanchthon favored the eucharistic prayer. But, as Armand Boehme has pointed out, that is the opposite of what he taught.[158] In fact, he called it a "wicked thing." "The controversy about the canon was very important to me," Melanchthon wrote, "and I give thanks that I am successful so that that wicked thing has not been demanded of the pastors."[159] For him, preventing use of the eucharistic prayer was the same as saving the Reformation.

> The action at Leipzig makes no change in the church because the contention concerning the mass and the eucharistic prayer is postponed for further consideration.[160]

Etymology

Liturgy (*Leiturgia*), does, in fact, as many writers insist, mean "the work of the people." In Greek, it means secular work done by a public official. That it was the word used by the Septuagint for the Old Testament temple cult, however, does not justify the arguments for human initiative in the sacrament. Good theology is not based on etymology.

---

157 *Wider das Interim, Papistische Mess, Canonem, und Meister Eisleuben durch Christianum Lauterwar, zu dieser Zeit nützlich zu lesen* (Magdeburg: Michael Lotter, 1549), A iv v.

158 "Does it or Doesn't it? Apology XXIV and Eucharistic Prayers." *Logia: A Journal of Lutheran Theology* 13 (2004): 11-20; Oliver K. Olson, "Melanchthon on the Eucharistic Prayer," *Lutheran Quarterly* 19 (2005): 199-207.

159 CR 7:341f.

160 CR 8:297.

For him [Melancthon], preventing use of the eucharistic prayer was the same as saving the Reformation.

The same is true of the word *worship*, whose etymology also points to human effort, "giving worth." More satisfactory are the words *Gottesdienst* and *service*, which can mean either our service to God (incorrect), or his service to us (correct).

Ecumenical Consensus

Exactly what is ecumenical consensus? The word *consensus* can be appealing to those who cherish *concordia*. The evangelical Lutheran *concordia*, however, is printed in black and white for everyone to read in the Book of Concord. But ecumenical consensus on the liturgy is not an honest term. Appeals to that consensus are arbitrary. Why should we accept such a vague authority? Who is doing the consenting? For one thing, it is apparent that ecumenical is not quite exact. Examination of the three successive hymnals suggests that the consensus does not include Presbyterians or Methodists, say, but only Episcopalians and Roman Catholics.

Which should it be? The (ecumenical) *Church's* Supper, or the *Lord's* Supper? Our eucharist dare not be mixed in the Sacrament of the Altar with God's gift to us.

The Sacrament Turned Upside-Down

Once, evangelical Lutherans understood that God was the initiator of the sacrament. But that was before "ecumenical consensus" and the mountain of books and articles that convinced the liturgically-minded that man is initiator.

> A disturbing question is why *Evangelical Lutheran Worship* prefers the notions of *eucharist* and *covenant* (*ELW,* 108) to *testament*. Both those words describe something people do. "The first abuse of the mass is this," Luther wrote (*LW* 35:92), "that we have lost the chief blessing, namely, the testament and faith."

Chapter 6 • The Eucharistic Prayer

Having surrendered to ecumenical authority our impressionable liturgy officials are turning the sacrament upside-down. Beginning with the mention in the *Service Book and Hymnal* of a "proper use of the eucharistic prayer" the Council of Trent has made great inroads into the Lutheran church (*SBH,* vii). According to Mark Chapman, a spokesman for the powerful new movement called "Evangelical–Catholicism":

> Whatever may be the case for other issues, the Reformation is over in regard to the form of the eucharistic liturgy and the Eucharistic Prayer has been restored and reformed.[161]

Chapman believes that to incarnate Jesus' words and make them effective, *human words are necessary.*

> His [Christ's] Words of Institution, set in the narrative of his life and Israel's life and his Church's life, emerge as the powerful and performative word of his holy promise made real and effective … *This is something that the Verba alone could never do* … Embodied in the dialogue of the Eucharistic Prayer, the Words of Institution became incarnate as the living Christ and his living Bride in holy conversation and communion. And that is salvation.

> The remembrance is what we bring to the Eucharist, and so is part of our sacrifice, our offering—of our tradition, our memory, our instruction, our scholarship, our upbringing of Christ, we lift up in prayer and praise the narrative that holds and hangs flesh on those Words of Institution.[162]

Such arguments, Martin Luther wrote, are "the babbling of the seditious spirits who, contrary to the Word of God, regard the sacraments as something that we do."[163]

161 "Fundamental Unity. Evangelical-Catholic Non-Negotiables," *Lutheran Forum,* Christmass [sic] (2005): 13.

162 "The Eucharistic Prayer in Lutheran Liturgy," *The Bride of Christ* 15 (1991): 25 [emphasis added].

163 The Large Catechism, Fifth Part, The Sacrament of the Altar [BC, 467].

Such arguments, Martin Luther wrote, are "the babbling of the seditious spirits who, contrary to the Word of God, regard the sacraments as something that we do."

For Discussion

1. Why does the church keep on using Greek words?

2. What is the meaning of these Greek words, *adiaphora, epiclesis,* and *anamnesis*?

3. Is there such a thing as a "Christian Seder"?

4. What is meant by the observation that the whole papacy is in canon?

5. How is the eucharistic prayer politically conservative?

Chapter 7

Reclaiming Christ's Testament

There Is No "Proper Use" of the Prayer of Thanksgiving

The harmlessness of consecrating by giving thanks was assumed in the November 2006 issue of *The Lutheran* magazine, in which Robert Rimbo compared the sacrament to the Thanksgiving holiday.

> For November it's appropriate to think about "eucharist," that funny word that means "thanksgiving." In the meal Jesus said, "Do this," But have you ever asked: "Do what?" … I think more central to what Jesus did in his institution of this sacred meal and more central to our gatherings is thanksgiving."[164]

As we have seen above, in contrast to the *Service Book and Hymnal* or what anyone "thinks," the confessional Lutheran position is that "Do this" is not a mandate for prayer—any kind of prayer (*SBH*, vii).

The shadowy "ecumenical consensus" is not available officially in a document anywhere. For what it is we have to rely on is the word of the initiated. One such sighting is reported in the same article in *The Lutheran* magazine.

> There are [sic] now an immense array of eucharistic prayers. But each has these elements: They start off praising God and then different memories are evoked as promptings for this thanksgiving. They remind God and us that we do this in memory [*anamnesis*] of Jesus. They ask God to send the Spirit [*epiclesis*] upon us and our gifts so we may be drawn more and more into unity with God and one another.

164 Robert Rimbo, "Worship Whys: Thanksgiving," *The Lutheran*, November 2006, 61.

> … the confessional Lutheran position is that "Do this" is not a mandate for prayer—any kind of prayer.

He is not alone. Frank Senn has the same standard in mind. In spite of the almost complete lack of information about the early history of the liturgy, he asserts that there was a "classical shape" and a "patristic synthesis."

> I want a eucharistic prayer of classical shape with all the elements of the patristic synthesis included—praise to the Father with proper preface leading to the Sanctus, remembrance of the Son including "on the night in which he was betrayed ..." invocation of the Spirit leading to the commemoration of all the saints and a concluding Trinitarian doxology.[165]

Principles for Worship assures us that "the whole meal is a great thanksgiving" (*PW,* 8). *Lutheran Book of Worship* calls the prayer the "Great Thanksgiving" (*LBW,* 68). *Evangelical Lutheran Worship* agrees (*ELW,* 107, 129, etc.).

Post-communion prayers of thanksgiving are "eucharist." Helping an old lady across the street on Thursday afternoon is "eucharist." Visiting a wretched prisoner is "eucharist." The Lord's Supper is not "eucharist."

Lutheran Liturgical Education

Students learn about "eucharist" from professors of liturgy in ELCA seminaries. So, we have a crisis on our hands, about which members of seminary boards should be concerned. According to the Anglican Brian Spinks of the Yale Institute of Sacred Music:

> But, if nothing else, Lutherans should not be intimidated by the oversimplification of modern popular liturgical writings, and perhaps need to develop their own strong academic liturgical programs rather than leaving the American field to the Roman Catholic universities and seminaries.[166]

Gift Character

The *Service Book and Hymnal* recommended "proper use of the Prayer of Thanksgiving" (*SBH,* vii). But since it reverses the direction of the sacrament there is no "proper use." Luther's pastor, liturgical specialist Johann

---

Synonyms:
Canon of the mass
Mass canon
Eucharistic prayer
Great Thanksgiving
The Prayer of Thanksgiving

---

165 Email correspndence from Frank C. Senn, November 6, 2006.

166 Brian Spinks, "Berakah, Anaphoral Theory and Luther," *Lutheran Quarterly* III (1989): 279.

Chapter 7 • Reclaiming Christ's Testament

Bugenhagen, also warned against the change of direction of the words of institution. "To make a prayer of it would be a *human interference in the command, and is therefore forbidden.*"[167]

Matthias Flacius, agreed:

> … the work which God shows to men, that he has created, renews, upholds us and promises eternal life, cannot be called a sacrifice of thank-offering.[168]

> Who cannot understand that this name, eucharist, or thanksgiving, does not properly pertain to the sacrament of the altar? For in this fashion, the meal of every Christian could be called "eucharist," since before and after eating he gives thanks to God the Lord for his benefits, and every common prayer and thanksgiving of the churches can rightly be called "eucharist," even when no distribution or giving of the sacrament occurs.[169]

From the pulpit, in contrast, it should be emphasized that every thanksgiving prayer, every good work done out of thankfulness to God is "eucharist." Flacius continues:

> It is more accurate to call the sacrament communion, a work whereby our Lord God shows himself gracious toward us, for just as in Christ's stead the minister baptizes, absolves and comforts in the name of Jesus, he also offers us his body and blood, in order that we receive the communion from him and not that (as occurs in the mass) we sacrifice. That is what the words of the meal clearly imply.

> We do not sacrifice, but receive it. The words of institution imply that one does not sacrifice, but receives, just as it is God who baptizes, absolves, and comforts with the Holy Gospel. In the sacrament of the altar, it is he who offers us his body and blood. As the word of God, it cannot be called men's sacrifice any more than can absolution and baptism.

In Sweden Ragnar Bring warned us.

> If there is the slightest thought that Communion is an offering to God, a sacred act in God's direction, then the Gospel is rendered null and void at once.[170]

---

167 *Die Reform der Messliturgie durch Johannes Bugenhagen* (Kevelaier, Germany, 1966), 214 [emphasis added].

168 *Wider das Interim*, B ij v.

169 *Von der Hailigsten Messe*, (Ingolstadt: Wiessenhorn, 1548), C r.

170 "On the Lutheran Concept of the Sacrament," *World Lutheranism of Today: A Tribute to Anders Nygren*, (Stockholm: Svenska Kyrkans Diakonistyrelses Bokförlag, 1936), 54.

"To make a prayer of it [words of institution] would be a *human interference in the command, and is therefore forbidden.*"

From the pulpit, in contrast, it should be emphasized that every thanksgiving prayer, every good work done out of thankfulness to God is "eucharist."

In Germany Dorothea Wendebourg wrote:

> The flattening-out of the Words of Institution into that thanksgiving ... leads to the loss of the gift-character of the sacrament.[171]

In Norway Carl Wislöff wrote:

> Whereas the Lord's Supper, according to the Words of Institution, is purely a gift of God, the mass had been turned into a kind of performance on the part of man. Here, where God himself sets the table and everything is completely prepared that, on our part, nothing else is asked than a thirsty soul, humility, and readiness to receive....[172]

In 1960 the ULCA ruled that:

> ... the sacrament cannot be called "eucharist," or "thanksgiving" ... The essential nature of the sacrament is gift (*beneficium*). The direction is altogether from God to man.[173]

In 1974, commenting on *LBW*, the official American Lutheran Church (ALC) Review Group ruled that:

> While we appreciate the efforts of ILCW to bring us into a more ecumenical celebration of the Sacrament, we think that it obscures the Lutheran contribution to the understanding of the Sacrament. We are not convinced that it represents a healthy development within the worship life of the church ... the proclamatory nature of the Words of Institution is hidden, if not lost completely; the epiclesis is offensive in its suggestion that something unique happens to the elements when the Holy Spirit is invoked; the bringing of gifts of money with the bread and wine obscures God's great gift to us.[174]

Our Changeable Church

Whom shall we believe? The ULCA and ALC or an unsupervised committee? In 1960 the Lutheran church was still faithful to the Book of Concord; in 2006 it has wandered off to "ecumenical consensus." In 1960 it taught that the Lord's Supper was Christ's "testament"; in 2006 the *ELW* says it is our giving thanks. In 1960 the direction of the sacrament was still downward, with God as initiator. A half century later the direction is upward, with the church as initiator, with the excuse that it is "thanksgiving."

---

[171] "Noch einmal 'Den falschen Weg Roms zu Ende gegangen'"? *Zeitschrift für Theologie und Kirche* 99 (2002), 405.

[172] "C. Fr. Wislöff, "Gottesdienst und Opfer," *Lutherische Rundschau* 5 (1955/56): 373.

[173] "The Sacrament of the Altar and Its Implications: Statement adopted by the 1960 Convention of the United Lutheran Church in America as a Guide to Its Congregations," *Liturgical Reconnaissance: Papers Presented at the Inter-Lutheran Consultation on Worship, February 10-11, 1966* (Philadelphia: Fortress Press, 1968), 38.

[174] Letter to President David Preus from Omar Bonderud, March 16, 1976 (Chicago: ELCA Archives).

Chapter 7 • Reclaiming Christ's Testament

The venerable words *evangelical* and *Lutheran* are not to be found on the cover of the new hymnal. The cranberry-red spine bears only one word, *Worship*. Appropriately so, since the basic direction of the *ELW* is neither "evangelical" nor "Lutheran."

With the Whole Church, the *Renewing Worship Study* does relapse a couple of times into Lutheranism. It states (correctly) that "God alone is the actor in baptism and communion."[175] And *Evangelical Lutheran Worship* reprints the catechism's question, "What is the benefit of such eating and drinking?" And the answer, "forgiveness of sin" (*ELW*, 1166). But, in the end, the emphases on human initiative, human "eucharist," win out.

What kind of changeable outfit is the Lutheran church, anyway, and *why should we believe anything it says?*

Navigating the *ELW*

The answer is: No matter what hymn books say and what the hierarchy promotes, we must follow the Confessions. Pastors who are serious about their ordination vow should be careful how they use the ELCA's new hymnal resource. They must use option II—bare verba—for communion (*ELW*, 108, 130) or the Service of the Word (*ELW*, 210). Preaching to communicants, they must insist that the proper preparation for taking communion is not arrogant "joy," but repentance. (Joy is not the precondition for communing, but the *result*.)

Conscientious pastors obviously will also refuse to read the heretical prayers for the dead or permit the use of any of the altered psalms or the readings from the Apocrypha. In addition, if they agree with Luther, they will avoid unnecessary ceremonies. They will resist "sprinkling" of water, lest holy water again incubate superstition. Against the tendency to make the participation of the "assembly" necessary in baptism, they will schedule some baptisms outside the Sunday service. Instead of Affirmation of Baptism, faithful pastors will duplicate other orders for confirmation.

They will also think carefully before using ceremonies of affirmation, as in Affirmation of Christian Vocation (*ELW*, 84) and Affirmation of

[175] *With the Whole Church: Renewing Worship Study Guide* (Minneapolis: Augsburg Fortress, 2005), 44.

Joy is not the precondition for communing, but the *result*.

Baptism (*ELW*, 234), knowing that affirmation suggests an (un-Lutheran) emphasis on freedom of the will. Moreover, there is no serious significance in a ceremony of affirmation! The curious ceremonies of Welcome to Baptism, Thanksgiving for Baptism, and imposition of ashes (*ELW*, 254), while harmless, are unneeded.

Frequency of Communion

According to *Evangelical Lutheran Worship* (*ELW*, 210), "a weekly celebration of the Lord's supper is the norm." But there is no norm, either in the Bible or by some survey since most Lutheran churches have not joined the movement toward communion every week. Augsburg Confession 24.34, Apology 15.40 and 24.1 report on communion every week,[176] but those passages in a context concerned with reducing the number of masses are historical reports and cannot be taken as a norm.

The Lutheran tradition of "ante-communion," ending before the consecration, rose out of the opposition to solitary masses (ridiculed as *Winkelmessen*, "masses in a corner"). The celebrants did not consecrate the elements when no communicants were expected.

How often should Holy Communion be offered? It is clear that in the Roman Catholic Church, which promotes not just weekly, but daily celebrations, almost all interest is concentrated on the mass. Lutherans should be watchful lest the movement toward weekly communion lessens confidence that God meets us in his preached Word.

---

176 Augsburg Confession 24.34; Apology 15.40, 24.1 [BC 71, 229, 285].

How often should Holy Communion be offered? ... Lutherans should be watchful lest the movement toward weekly communion lessens confidence that God meets us in his preached Word.

Chapter 7 • Reclaiming Christ's Testament

The *ReClaim* Hymnal

After fifty years of shadowy ecumenical consensus, Anglican four-action shape, and the vague, unexplained *ELW* process, we need a faithful hymnal. *ReClaim* is that book. Honoring ancient piety and determined to preserve continuity, it does provide three biblically-based orders of monastic origin—matins, vespers, and compline—for gatherings. More important, however, whereas the monks concentrated on separated communities, the Reformation's high view of marriage and family sparked interest in the workaday world and in daily worship in the home. Hence the name: *ReClaim: Lutheran Hymnal for Church and Home*.

Not wordy, it defers to the Word. "Ecumenical authority" to the contrary, its premise is that *God alone is the actor*. By omitting the offertory ceremony, it is boldly evangelical. And eliminating the eucharistic prayer as well, it carefully distinguishes what is required by the the liturgical command, "This do," and subordinates "Do this" to Jesus' evangelical promise, "For you."

"Ponder, then," Luther advised, "and include yourself personally in the you so that He may not speak to you in vain."[177]

177 Ibid., [BC].

... we need a faithful hymnal. *ReClaim* is that book.

For Discussion

1. What is the meaning of "testament"?

2. What should our reaction be if (when!) the church's doctrine changes?

3. How often should Holy Communion be celebrated?

4. What should be in our minds when we prepare to take communion?

Abbreviations

ALC   The American Lutheran Church

BC   Book of Concord

ELCA   Evangelical Lutheran Church in America

ELCIC   Evangelical Lutheran Church in Canada

ELW   *Evangelical Lutheran Worship,* © Evangelical Lutheran Church in America (Minneapolis: Augsburg Fortress, Publishers, 2006).

ILCW   Inter-Lutheran Commission on Worship

LBW   *Lutheran Book of Worshp,* © Lutheran Church in America, The American Lutheran Church, The Evangelical Lutheran Church of Canada, The Lutheran Church–Missouri Synod (Minneapolis: Augsburg Publishing House; Philadelphia: Board of Publication, Lutheran Church in America, 1978).

LC–MS   Lutheran Church–Missouri Synod

LW   *Luther's Works: American Edition,* Jaroslav Pelikan and Helmut T. Lehmann, eds., 55 volumes (St. Louis: Concordia; Philadelphia: Fortress [Muhlenberg], 1955–1986).

PW   *Renewing Worship, Vol. 2: Principles for Worship,* © Evangelical Lutheran Church in America (Minneapolis: Augsburg Fortress, 2002).

SBH   *Service Book and Hymnal,* © The American Evangelical Lutheran Church, The American Lutheran Church, The Augustana Evangelical Lutheran Church, The Evangelical Lutheran Church, The Finnish Evangelical Lutheran Church in America, The Lutheran Free Church, The United Evangelical Lutheran Church, The United Lutheran Church in America (Minneapolis: Augsburg Publishing House; Philadelphia: Board of Publication Lutheran Church in America, 1958).

ULCA   The United Lutheran Church in America

WA   *D. Martin Luthers Werke: Kritische Gesamtausgabe,* 61 vols., (Weimar: Hermann Böhlaus Nachfolger, 1883-1983).

WOV   *With One Voice: A Lutheran Resource for Worship,* Pew Edition (Minneapolis: Augsburg Fortress, 1995).

Glossary of Terms

adiaphora	From Stoic philosophy; those matters that are indifferent; this concept became important to Lutherans in the sixteenth century during the Adiaphorist Controversy; singular: adiaphoron
anamnesis	Greek for memory or memorial
asperges	Ceremony of applying or sprinkling holy water
Augsburg Interim	Imperial Law of 1548 designed to force the Lutherans back into papal obedience
bare verba	See verba
canon of the mass	Canon means rule, as in "biblical canon"; the mass canon is the central prayer of the Roman Catholic mass, regulated by a rule (a canon); also called eucharistic prayer, mass canon, Prayer of Thanksgiving, Great Thanksgiving
catechization	A system of instructing young persons in the faith
concommitant acts	Acts that are unnecessary for sacrament to be valid
confect	To perform; used by Anglicans, as in the expression, to "confect" the sacrament
consecration	The act of blessing the elements, bread and wine, of communion
Didache	An early Christian manual on morals and church practice, with some evidence of sacramental usages
ecumenical	From Greek, *oikoumene*, "the inhabited world"; used to refer to commonality among Christian denominations
epiclesis	A prayer invoking the Holy Spirit
eschatological	Having to do with the Last Things
eucharistic prayer	See canon of the mass
eucharistic procession	Ceremonial presentation of the communion elements
evangelical catholic movement	A movement among Lutherans stressing similarities with Roman Catholics
formal acts	Things that are necessary, or needed, for a sacrament to be valid

Glossary of Terms

fraction	Breaking of the bread in the communion service
gnesio-Lutheran	True Lutheran; from Greek, gnesios; opposed the party of the "Philippists"; followers of Philipp Melanchthon
Great Thanksgiving	Another term for eucharistic prayer
historical critical method	A learned way of Bible study, using secular techniques
historic episcopate	The teaching that every bishop was consecrated by another bishop in a chain begun by Saint Peter
Lateran Council, Fourth	A church council (1215 A.D.) that introduced philosophical ideas of Aristotle into the church, including the notion of "transubstantiation"
Leipzig Interim	A 1548 catholicizing law of Saxony to regulate religion
lex orandi, lex credendi	The law of prayer is the law of believing
liturgy	The order of the Christian communion service
Liturgical Renewal Movement	A movement across several denominations marked by historical study and emphasis on early Christian worship practices
mass canon	See canon of the mass
monstrance	An open or transparent vessel made of gold or silver, to show the "host" (altar bread) to worshipers
Nihil Rule	There is no sacrament outside the use, or practice, which was instituted by Christ; see Formula of Concord, Solid Declaration, Article VII:85
offertory ritual	Ceremonial giving to the church
ontological change	Alteration of being; applied to ordination it means not only that an office is being transferred, but that the very being of the candidate is changed
ordinary	Invariable parts of the service, that is, Kyrie, Gloria, Nicene Creed, Sanctus, Agnus Dei
papistic	Matters related to the pope
propers	Variable parts of the service, such as the readings
real presence of Christ	The belief that in the sacrament of the altar Christ is present
receptionism	The understanding of the Lord's Supper that Christ is present only when the communicant receives the bread and wine
representatio, doctrine of	A new doctrine of the Roman Catholic Church, that in the mass, Jesus' death is made contemporary
transubstantiation	The belief that after consecration by a priest, Christ is permanently present in the altar bread
Trent, Council of	A council of the Roman Catholic Church (1545–1563), the first after the Reformation
Vatican II	A council of the Roman Catholic Church (1962–1965) that initiated many liturgical changes
verba	Latin for *word*; often refers to Jesus' words of institution (1 Cor. 11.23-26; Matt. 26.26-29; Mark 14.22-25; Luke 22.14-20) Also, bare verba